I0165866

THE GOLDEN BAND

FROM

TIGERLAND

The Hill Collection

HOLDINGS OF THE LSU LIBRARIES

The 1899 band and cadets in formation near the Pentagon Barracks at the old downtown campus, where the Tiger Band was born in November 1893. (LSUPC)

THE GOLDEN BAND

FROM

TIGERLAND

A HISTORY OF LSU'S MARCHING BAND

TOM CONTINÉ AND FAYE PHILLIPS | FOREWORD BY FRANK B. WICKES

LOUISIANA STATE UNIVERSITY PRESS | BATON ROUGE

Published by Louisiana State University Press
Copyright © 2016 by Louisiana State University
   Press
All rights reserved
Manufactured in China
First printing

Designer: Michelle A. Neustrom
Typefaces: Sentinel, text; Bebas Kai, display
Printer and binder: Everbest Printing Co. through
   Four Colour Imports, Ltd., Louisville, Kentucky

Unless otherwise credited, all photographs before
page 1 are by Rachel Saltzberg.

Library of Congress Cataloging-in-Publication Data
Names: Continé, Tom. | Phillips, Faye.
Title: The Golden Band from Tigerland : a history
   of LSU's marching band / Tom Continé and Faye
   Phillips ; foreword by Frank B. Wickes.
Description: Baton Rouge : Louisiana State Univer-
   sity Press, [2016] | Includes bibliographical refer-
   ences and index.
Identifiers: LCCN 2016009622| ISBN 978-0-8071-
   6350-4 (cloth : alk. paper) | ISBN 978-0-8071-
   6351-1 (pdf) | ISBN 978-0-8071-6352-8 (epub) |
   ISBN 978-0-8071-6353-5 (mobi)
Subjects: LCSH: Louisiana State University (Baton
   Rouge, La.). Tiger Marching Band—History.
Classification: LCC ML28.B265 T544 2016 | DDC
   784.8/306076318—dc23 LC record available at
   http://lccn.loc.gov/2016009622

The paper in this book meets the guidelines for
permanence and durability of the Committee on
Production Guidelines for Book Longevity of the
Council on Library Resources. ∞

TO ALL MEMBERS OF THE TIGER BAND:
PAST, PRESENT, AND FUTURE

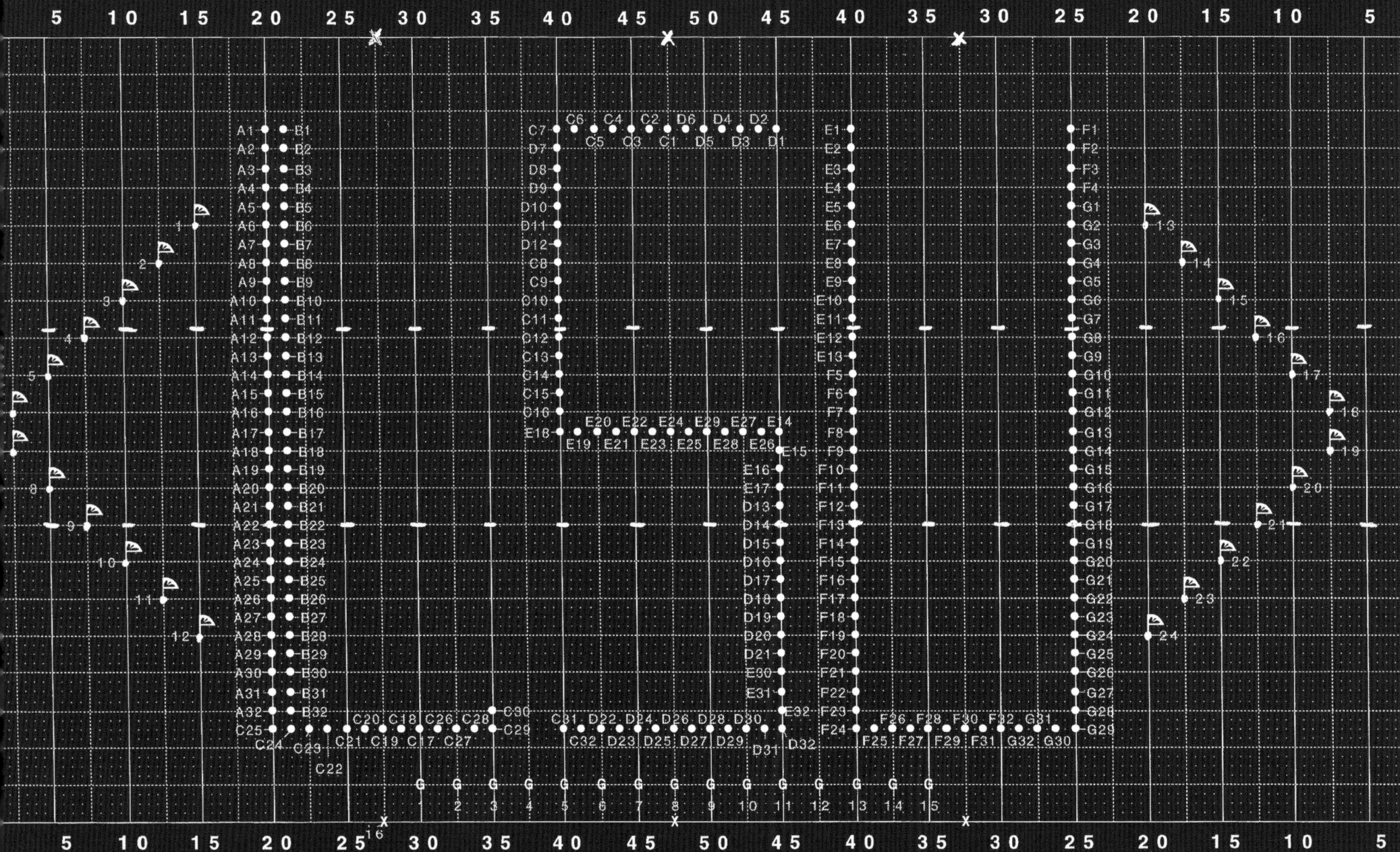

CONTENTS

FOREWORD

The first time I saw the LSU Tiger Marching Band was on October 6, 1973, when, as the newly appointed director of bands at the University of Florida, I traveled to Baton Rouge with the full Gator Band for the annual University of Florida–LSU football game. Seated in the southeast corner of Tiger Stadium, I watched the Tiger Band take the field for its pregame show. The crowd noise started to build with the sound of the drums. When the crowd erupted as the Tiger Band played to each corner, I turned to my assistant and said, "They've got tradition." Little did I know that just seven years later I would accept the job as director of bands at LSU and begin a thirty-year love affair with one of the most storied college marching bands in America.

In the southern United States, there is probably no more dominating social culture during the fall season than intercollegiate football. Millions of fans and millions of dollars are engaged in the excitement of Game Day and the televised pursuit of conference and national championships. Closely intertwined with the schools' teams are the longstanding traditions of the college and university marching bands that provide ceremonial music at pregame, entertainment at halftime, and rousing nonstop musical cheers during the game itself. At LSU, however, it's a cut above, and the band seems joined at the heart with the team, the fans, the alums, and the students. It is a special relationship that exists in few other places.

The musical traditions of the Tiger Marching Band run long and deep. The Golden Band from Tigerland is simply one of the best in America and has been for a long time, with awards to prove it. It began as a cadet band in 1893 with a student named Ruffin G. Pleasant as its first director; Pleasant went on to become governor of Louisiana. When populist governor Huey P. Long was elected in 1928, he collaborated with Alfred Wickboldt and Castro Carazo to transform the band into one of the largest in the country.

On football game day in the two hours before kickoff, it's the Tiger Band that generates the spirit among the fans and stirs their emotional fervor. Thousands line North Stadium Drive to watch the team and the band parade "Down the Hill" and greet fans with the "Pregame Salute." The Tiger Band then marches to the Pete Maravich Assembly Center to serenade three thousand more Tiger Athletic Foundation boosters with popular tunes and LSU school songs. Finally arriving in its seats in Tiger Stadium, the band plays another thirty minutes for the student body while the team warms up. Then comes the exit from the stands to the south end zone to line up for the Tiger Band's nationally famous pregame show. The noise level rises to fever pitch as the band plays to both sides of the stadium. Then it marches downfield to form a human tunnel, where it delivers a spirited welcome to the Tiger football players as they run onto the field. Now we're ready for kickoff!

This book is a tribute to the thousands of Tiger Band students and their directors who have given so much to LSU and worked so hard to produce the musical and marching excellence that helped build the traditions and reputation of the Golden Band from Tigerland. Long may it live! Geaux Tigers!

—Frank B. Wickes
Director of Bands, LSU
1980–2010

ACKNOWLEDGMENTS

The authors wish to thank Florence Jumonville, our friend and colleague, who served as first reader, proofreader, fact checker, copyeditor, and indexer. She made it possible for us to complete a book worthy of its subject. LSU Band photographer Rachel Saltzberg is a wonderful artist who shared her brilliant photographs. Aided by other talented and patient LSU Press staff, Margaret Lovecraft brought the book from idea to life. Many photographers, librarians, archivists, writers, students, friends, and families lent their talents and thoughts, and sometimes prayers.

In particular we also wish to acknowledge Mike Nelson, Charlie Roberts, Dawson Corley, Pat Wafer, Susan Moreau, Randy Smith, Dorothy Smith, Larry Hubbard, Nina Snapp, Florent Hardy, Tom Fronek, John Sibley Butler, Michael Strasser, Ron Ross, Johnny Gordon, Barry Cowan, Judy Bolton, Roy King, Linda Saucier, Mary Bahlinger, Stephen Koivisto, and Frank B. Wickes.

THE GOLDEN BAND

FROM

TIGERLAND

Although it bears no identifying date, this may be the earliest official photograph of the Cadet Band. It is the only existing band photo with just nine members shown. Barrow and Ruffin are perhaps missing from the group. (LSUPC)

1

FROM HUMBLE BEGINNINGS
1893–1930

Today's renowned Golden Band from Tigerland stands in stark contrast to the handful of Ole War Skule cadets who joined together over a century ago to create a brass band for their alma mater. Drably uniformed and numbering just eleven, those young men could not possibly have imagined that their band would evolve into an icon so beloved and so rich in tradition that its mere entry onto the field of Tiger Stadium rouses thousands of frenzied spectators to their feet in roaring approval.

This image, taken by Andrew Lytle around 1897–1898, shows Wylie M. Barrow in the dark suit to the left, and Ruffin G. Pleasant in the dark suit near the center, with band members. By this time, Barrow was a Baton Rouge businessman and Pleasant was a member of the LSU faculty. The drum is painted "Cadet Parade Band." (LSUPC)

THE FIRST DECADE

Louisiana State University, an all-male military institution with an enrollment of fewer than two hundred young cadets, was located on the grounds of the future site of the "new" state capitol building, several blocks north of Baton Rouge's town center. In 1893, two upperclassmen, Wylie M. Barrow and Ruffin G. Pleasant, announced their intention of organizing a brass band on campus. Word quickly spread among the student body, and nine cadets answered the call. The group held its first meeting early on the evening of November 20, 1893, in the university's Pentagon Barracks complex. In attendance were Barrow, Pleasant, J. A. Blouin, W. P. Cooper, J. M. Huey, J. Joumel, F. Lyons, W. S. Maguire, J. E. Morris, A. Rain, and N. S. Trichel.

Apparently, the band's co-organizers impressed their fellow cadets favorably, because Barrow was selected to serve as president and Pleasant was chosen to lead the band. Whether any other business was transacted at the initial meeting is unknown, but since all of the cadets assembled decided to take part in the enterprise, it seems that Barrow and Pleasant succeeded in selling the idea to their fellow students. Many of the band's charter members went on to achieve prominence in their chosen fields. Among them, Wylie Macajah Barrow (1874–1934) became a prosperous attorney and businessman in Baton Rouge. Ruffin Golson Pleasant (1871–1937), from Shreveport, served as governor of Louisiana from 1916 to 1920.

From its inception, the Cadet Band, as it came to be called, received a measure of moral support, encouragement, and limited financial assistance from the school's administration. It had no inventory of school-owned instruments, no equipment, no music library, no special uniforms, and no place of its own in which to rehearse, but what it did have would prove to be more important to its long-term survival than the things it lacked. The band began its existence with a pair of determined, dedicated founders and a small cadre of eager, enthusiastic cadets. The combination proved to be more than sufficient.

THE FIRST DIRECTOR

Pleasant served as the Cadet Band's student leader until his graduation in 1896. After completing one year of study at Yale University Law School, he returned to LSU as a full-time member of the faculty. During Pleasant's absence from LSU, W. B. Clarke directed the band while holding a full-time teaching position at the Louisiana State

This is the first known published photograph of the band. It appeared in the Fall 1895–Spring 1896 *LSU Catalog*. The band is to the left of the battalion of cadets. (LSUPC)

School for the Blind. Clarke, blind himself, was a highly talented cornet player and musician.

When he returned to LSU, in addition to his teaching assignments, Pleasant served as assistant commandant of cadets, manager of the football team for 1897–1898, and director of the Cadet Band. He satisfied the demands of these diverse responsibilities for one school term and then decided that in fairness to his students and to the university, he should devote his time and energy to his teaching and administrative duties. Consequently, in 1898 Pleasant voluntarily, though reluctantly, resigned as leader of the Cadet Band.

A FULL-TIME DIRECTOR

Charles A. Kellogg (b. ca. 1870) followed Pleasant as director of the Cadet Band. He received a full-time faculty appointment, allowing him to focus exclusively on the organization's growth and musical development. The school administration recognized the band's value to the institution and demonstrated a willingness to provide increasing

Band on the parade ground at the old campus, ca. 1903. (LSUPC)

financial support. By the turn of the century, the band had become one of the most popular organizations on campus. Its musicianship had greatly improved under Kellogg's leadership, and it received more invitations to perform at campus and local events than it could accept.

Prior to 1900, each bandsman was expected to furnish his own instrument, and few exceptions were made. Most cadets, however, could not afford to purchase the larger, more expensive brass instruments needed to balance the growing band's instrumentation. The university administration recognized this impediment to the band's development and assumed the responsibility of providing these types of instruments without charge to band members. This initiated a school-owned inventory of musical instruments, another important step for the Cadet Band. According to the *LSU Catalog, 1899–1900,* the band was a voluntary activity with instruments supplied by the university unless the cadet preferred to own the instrument he used. Every band member paid a fee of one dollar per month until 1903, when the fee rose to four and a half dollars.[1]

A MARCHING BAND

Shortly after the band's organizational meeting in 1893, Cadet F. Lyons was selected as its first drum major. Nothing is known about his qualifications for the position, but a drum major is usually chosen for musical and marching ability and for strength of leadership. Since the Cadet Band did not engage in marching activities until 1900, Lyons's function as drum major remains a mystery. News sources of the late 1890s reported that the band frequently provided musical entertainment for local events but never commented on it as a marching unit—but change was in the air. At some point during the 1900–1901 school year, officers of LSU's Military Department called upon Kellogg and the band to provide martial music for the Corps of Cadets as it drilled and marched in military revues and parades. At first, the forty-member band simply stood at attention in block formation and played as the cadets passed by, but before long it was also marching. LSU had its first marching band, led by its first marching, uniformed drum major. Because of LSU's strict military tradition, it was inappropriate for the band's drum major to twirl and spin his baton or display any "showmanship." Three decades later, a flamboyant governor would transform the drum major into a dazzling spectacle of glitter and glitz whose function became to amaze and enthrall the crowds of onlookers as much as to lead the band.

Perhaps because of the new importance placed on the band by LSU's Military Department, Kellogg's impressiveness as band director, or the improved quality of the bandsmen's performance, in 1902 Baton Rouge businessmen made generous donations to the Cadet Band. Thanked in official university publications for their gifts were William Garig, for a silver-plated tuba; S. I. Reymond, for a silver-plated four-valve euphonium; Rosenfield Dry Goods Company, for a silver-plated trombone; Fuqua Hardware Company, for a B-flat clarinet; and J. Farrnbacher and Son, for an E-flat clarinet.[2]

Kellogg's five-year tenure as band director ended in May 1903. He achieved four important "firsts" for the university and its band: first full-time director, first school-owned inventory of instruments, and first marching band with the first marching drum major.

DISTINCTIVE UNIFORMS

Frank E. Miller (b. ca. 1882) was hired as LSU's band director for the fall 1903 semester. Although his tenure lasted for only one year, it is memorable for a significant milestone in the band's history. Since the band's founding in 1893, no special uniform had differentiated its members from other student cadets. Originally, all of the university's cadets wore a uniform designed by officers of the Military Department and modeled after the uniform of the United States Military Academy at West Point. LSU's uniform, like that of West Point, was gray with black trim. During Miller's tenure, the commandant of cadets and his officers decided that in some small way the bandsmen should be distinguished from other cadets. In 1904, the band's uniform sported white trim. The variation in color from black to white was indeed minute, but it served its intended purpose and set the band apart. This seemingly insignificant change was the first step in an evolution of style, color, and glitz that would characterize the band's uniforms for the next hundred years.

THE ST. LOUIS WORLD EXPOSITION

In 1904, D. P. West (b. ca. 1883) succeeded Miller as band director. West's time in the position, like that of his predecessor, was unremarkable except for one very special event. The thirty-four-member Cadet Band accompanied four companies of LSU's Corps of Cadets to St. Louis, Missouri, to represent the university and the state of Louisiana at the Louisiana Purchase Exposition of 1904. This was by far the longest and most extensive trip the band had ever made. In 1942 the *Baton Rouge Morning Advocate* retold the story of the St. Louis band trip. According to the article, the bandsmen and other members of the corps traveled to St. Louis in style and comfort on a special train chartered for them with funds appropriated by the Louisiana legislature.[3]

The modest hat and attire of the 1915 drum major would evolve into the elaborate and stunning displays seen in the 1930s. (LSUPC)

The band in 1909. (LSUPC)

W. B. CLARKE

When West's directorship of the LSU Band ended in 1906, W. B. Clarke, who had previously led the band during Pleasant's yearlong absence, returned to the job. Originally from Louisville, Kentucky, William Britt Clarke (1862–1933) was born with cataracts and was completely blind by age ten. He came to Baton Rouge in 1885 to teach at the Louisiana State School for the Blind, where he directed the Music Department for forty years. Clarke became the organist at St. James Episcopal Church as well. He married Julia Cornelia Edwards, also a teacher at the School for the Blind and a member of one of the earliest families to settle in Baton Rouge. As director of the Cadet Band for nine years, Clarke presided over its most productive early period.

Under Clarke's leadership, the band increased in size, the quality of its musical performance gradually improved, and its popularity with the university's student body reached a new high. In the first football game of the 1907 season against the Louisiana Institute from Ruston, LSU's Rooters Club headed by the university band "came on the field and marched up and down emitting lusty college yells." For the traditional Firemen's Day Parade and celebration of George Washington's birthday in February 1908, thousands of visitors from throughout the state watched the Corps of Cadets lead the parade with "the famous LSU band at their head." The *Baton Rouge Advocate* reported: "One of the features of the parade was the drum major. He caused a ripple of comment and admiration wherever the band appeared. He seemed to stand fully seven feet high and four feet wide." Certainly drum major P. D. Pary made an impression. The band had another chance to give a stunning performance in December 1908 when Baton Rouge celebrated LSU's first football Championship of the South with a formal parade led by LSU president Thomas Boyd, Louisiana governor J. Y. Sanders, Sr., and Baton Rouge mayor W. H. Bynum.[4]

In May 1910, Clarke and the Cadet Band traveled far from home to Memphis, Tennessee. For an elaborate celebration of the city's one-hundredth anniversary, the Memphis Centennial Commission invited cadet bands from southern colleges to participate in two parades and paid their expenses. Impressed by the quality of the LSU Band's musical performance and the discipline of its members, the *Memphis Commercial Appeal* commented, "The LSU Band entertained so well that it received highly favorable press and wild acclaim from all those who heard it."[5] Word of the Memphis media's high praise for the band apparently spread around campus and Baton Rouge, coming to the attention of LSU's administration. Before long, and perhaps as a result, the Cadet Band was officially recognized as an integral element in the fabric of university life. The

W. B. Clarke, sitting center front, with black trim on jacket, directed the LSU Cadet Band twice. (LSUPC)

school's fall 1910 register of classes listed the organization's rehearsal schedule for the first time since its inception. No longer an appendage of the greater body, it was now a vital part of the whole.

Undeterred by his blindness, Clarke seldom missed any of the band's performances, but, concerned for his safety and well-being, the bandsmen took turns assisting him each day. Clarke took great pleasure in playing his cornet along with the band in rehearsal and performance. His musicianship likely lent quite a boost to the sound of

The LSU Cadet Band's photograph in the 1917 *Gumbo*, probably taken in fall 1916 before the United States entered World War I in April 1917. (LSUPC)

the band, as well as to the spirit of its members. The 1913 *Gumbo* praised Clarke's and the Cadet Band's contribution to the university and its students, stating that no other single organization did more for LSU than the band as it traveled throughout the state. "Its services contribute materially to the enjoyment and success of athletics and other events at the University. Here's to the Band! Long may it blow!"

WORLD WAR I AND A BATTLE OF THE BAND

World War I had a profound impact on LSU, as it did on universities throughout the country. Faculty members left their academic posts to answer the nation's call, and many young cadets followed their example. Surprisingly, despite a decrease in LSU's student enrollment, the size of the Cadet Band remained constant, averaging thirty-four members through the war years (1917–1918 for America). When war began in 1914 in Europe, Clarke tailored the band's repertory to reflect the patriotic mood prevalent in the country, eliminating nearly all of the popular tunes favored by the student musicians and other cadets. It did not occur to him to consider the opinions and preferences of his bandsmen. The abrupt and drastic change in the band's musical fare precipitated the first student rebellion in the Cadet Band's history.

As the story goes, one afternoon in mid-January 1915, bandsmen held a secret meeting before regular rehearsal to discuss the "sorry state" of the recently revised repertory and to devise a strategy for correcting the travesty. It didn't take long for things to get out of hand. The cadets began burning the patriotic tunes that Clarke favored. When he unexpectedly appeared on the scene prepared for band practice, the musicians grabbed their instruments and burst into a rousing rendition of their favorite popular tune, "Rover Dog." Clarke angrily refused to allow it, and the Cadet Band went on strike from rehearsals and performances, demanding to play popular tunes. Clarke remained adamant and unyielding. The dispute became serious—a test of will between teacher and students. Ultimately, President Thomas Boyd intervened, and within a few days a compromise was reached.

To the bandsmen's delight, Clarke agreed to reinstate "Rover Dog," though patriotic tunes and military marches would continue to constitute the greater part of the band's repertory. The insurrection of LSU's Cadet Band was taken quite seriously at the time, but it was amicably settled with no lasting harm to the relationship between the director and his bandsmen. Clarke later recalled that he should have been prepared for the standoff, because when he first arrived on campus he was confronted with the band's rendition of a popular ragtime piece. They made such a noise, Clarke said, "I had to beat on the table to get them to stop and when I did they were highly indignant because I had 'killed it all.'" Lester Williams, who became a leading pillar of Baton Rouge society, said Clarke blasted their hopes for modern music.[6] Clarke's tenure as director of the university's cadet band ended with his return full-time to the Louisiana State School for the Blind in 1915.

NEW PROFESSIONAL LEADERSHIP

LSU's Department of Music was established in the fall of 1915, with Henry W. Stopher (1883–1947) as its first director. In addition to fulfilling administrative duties, he led the Cadet Band. Of those who had served as band director to that point, Stopher was the best educated. He had earned a teaching certificate at Indiana State Normal College and a bachelor of music degree at Cornell University. His teaching experience included two years as assistant instructor at Indiana State Normal and five years as director of public school music at Louisiana State Normal.

In Stopher's first year as director, the Cadet Band performed at the State Fair in Shreveport and in carnival parades in New Orleans. The band provided martial music for the Military Department's revues and parades, entertained at Tiger football games both at home and away, and performed at various campus and local events. It became one of the most visible and popular organizations of the university.

DEMILITARIZED BAND

Since its inception, the Cadet Band was officially called the Military Band, and marching became part of its job. Qualified students were allowed to substitute band membership for the military drill required of all students. The band's status changed in 1916 when the Reserve Officers Training Corps (ROTC) was established on the LSU campus, although it retained the name Cadet Band and still reported to the commandant of cadets. The *LSU Catalog* for that year stated: "The band as a military organization ceased to exist. This change in management, however, has in no wise affected the playing ability of the band and has affected the membership to only a slight degree. Although the band is not a military organization, marching is one of the features of the band work."[7]

FRANK T. GUILBEAU

At the close of spring term of 1918, Stopher took a leave of absence to work for the Young Men's Christian Association (YMCA) as part of the war effort. On his recommendation, President Boyd appointed Frank T. Guilbeau to take charge of the Music Department. After Stopher returned to LSU in September 1919, he felt it necessary to devote all of his energy to developing the Music Department and voluntarily relinquished leadership of the band. Guilbeau continued to direct it.[8]

Director Guilbeau stands to the far right with the 1928 band. (LSUPC)

Born in Breaux Bridge, Louisiana, Guilbeau (1868–1934) came to LSU around 1887 and lived in Baton Rouge the remainder of his life. Guilbeau's time as band director would last for twelve years, extending through the first two years of Huey P. Long's governorship. When Guilbeau was "retired" by Governor Long in 1930, he had served as LSU's band director longer than any of his predecessors.

Guilbeau's tenure began with an important development in the band's history. Since the organization's founding in 1893, each cadet had been required to furnish his own uniform. In 1918, the university administration assumed the responsibility to provide each bandsman with one complete dress uniform, free of charge. The uniforms, however, reverted to the same design worn by the Corps of Cadets. By 1923 the distinguishing white braid for the band uniforms was gone, and military-only attire prevailed until 1931. The precedent set in 1918 quickly evolved into university policy, and the school continues to supply the band's uniforms.

For years, the band's inventory of school-owned instruments had met its needs, although many of the instruments were old and in varying stages of chronic disrepair. Guilbeau received authorization from President Boyd to purchase several new instruments for the band. At the end of the 1919 school term, the value of the organization's inventory of instruments was estimated to exceed four thousand dollars, an impressive sum for the time. Guilbeau also appealed to Boyd for funds to extensively expand the band's music library. He compiled a comprehensive collection of music with a broad variety of pieces for wind instruments and percussion.

The move to LSU's new campus began in 1923 and continued for several years. By 1924, the band's membership had increased to approximately forty-four student musicians. The largest band in school history, it was smartly uniformed and well equipped. Local news reports claimed that it had no peer in Louisiana or, for that matter, in the entire South.

THE BIRTH OF THE HALFTIME SHOW

One of LSU's cherished football traditions is the Tiger Band's halftime extravaganza, which never fails to thrill with polished precision and awesome sound. Oddly, the band's first halftime performance was unplanned and unrehearsed. Some stories place the event at an away game during the November 1921 Shreveport State Fair. Visits by the band to the State Fair were regular occurrences, and it is well documented that the members often paraded from their hotel to the football field. That year, as in the past, the band played before the game and perhaps led a victory snake dance after the game. One story says that at halftime, "The band formed in a double column and bearing the Tiger [made of papier-mâché] at the head, paraded around the field to the 'Tiger Swing.'"[9]

According to other local lore, the first halftime show occurred several years later, in the just-completed football stadium on the new campus. In any case, it was that first halftime performance at home that truly began the tradition. It happened in 1924 when LSU played against Spring Hill College of Mobile. At the end of the second quarter, the LSU cheerleaders managed to entice the bandsmen to leave their seats in the stands and join them on the field. It is uncertain whether they had Guilbeau's permission to do so. Accepting the cheerleaders' challenge, the band mustered on the turf, struck up a tune, and proceeded to march the length of the field. Not to be outdone, a gang of noisy students joined in the impromptu parade, encouraging the band with choruses of wild cheers. The band played on, rambling down the field with the students following close behind. The halftime celebration ended without incident, almost as spon-

The Practice House, 1926. (JFP)

taneously as it had begun. Those present at that game could hardly have imagined that they witnessed the birth of a new, enduring tradition that in little more than a decade would mark the LSU Band as one of the nation's finest, and perhaps its very best.[10]

A HOME OF ITS OWN

Until the university moved to its present campus, the band had no permanent home. Over the years, various spaces, including the old military jail, had been provided for indoor rehearsals, but these had always been shared with sundry classes and organizations. In the process of relocating to the new campus, the school's administration felt that the time had finally come to construct a facility for the exclusive use of the band. In 1925, a one-story wood frame building of seventeen hundred square feet was completed. Located a short distance west of the new Pentagon Barracks, the "Practice House," as the bandsmen soon named it, consisted of a large rehearsal hall, a music library, two instrument storage rooms, and an office for the band director. By the standards of the day, the Practice House represented a huge step forward in the band's evolution. It was also one more indication of the value the LSU administration placed on the band's role in the life of the university.

In the final years of Guilbeau's tenure, band membership generally fluctuated between fifty and sixty cadet musicians but reached a high of eighty in the 1928–1929 school term. Guilbeau's impressive leadership ended with his resignation on December 1, 1930. On the very day Guilbeau resigned, Governor Huey P. Long introduced Alfred W. Wickboldt to the commandant of cadets, Major Troy H. Middleton, as LSU's new band director.

By 1930, the LSU Cadet Band had come of age. The dream of two young cadets had become reality. The Ole War Skule had its band, and a fine one at that! The stage was now set for Louisiana's enigmatic, flamboyant governor to chart a new course for the band he would adopt as his own, leading it to a complete transformation.

above: A farewell salute to the old campus, ca. 1925, as LSU begins its move to a larger site on Highland Road. (DMS)

right: Salute to the twenty-first century. (Photograph by Rachel Saltzberg)

Parade of champions, 2007. (LSU Band)

Performance in 2008. (LSU Band)

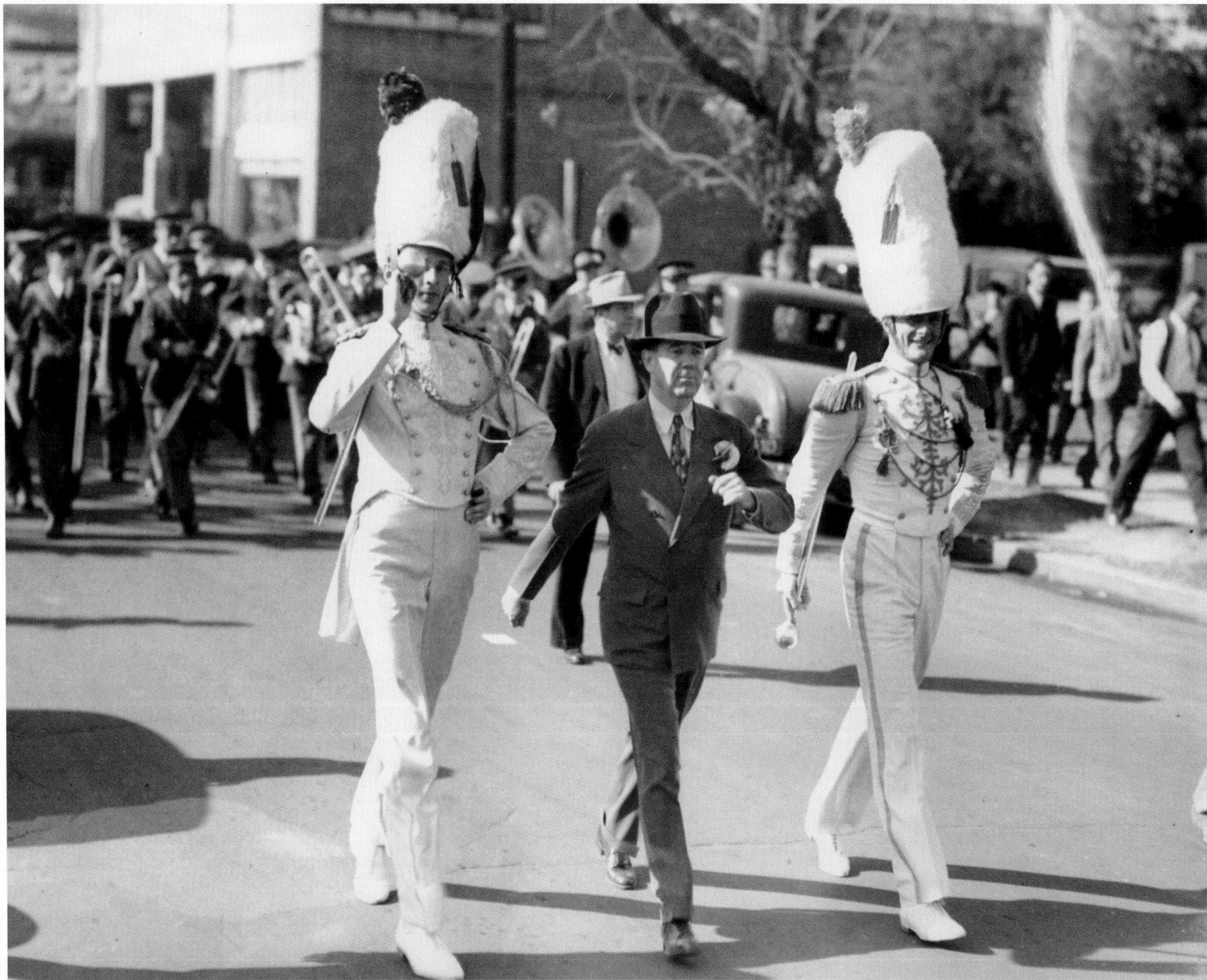

Huey Long took every opportunity to play the role of drum major and lead the LSU Band, as he did in 1934 with Lew Williams and Burns Bennett. (RBL)

2

THE GOVERNOR AND HIS BAND
1930–1940

Huey P. Long had an unabashed love affair with the LSU Band. He wanted to be involved with it in every possible way—from watching the band as it entertained crowds at LSU football games, to hearing it serenade onlookers from far and near, to writing songs for it and sometimes even conducting it in rehearsals. Most of all, he took great pride in leading the band in parades, marching at its head and alongside the drum major, at home and on trips. First as governor in 1928, then as United States senator in 1932, and until his assassination in 1935, he presided over the band's development, energizing it with unprecedented financial support. He was determined to remake the LSU Band into the largest and best university band in America. The reasons for Long's infatuation

Wickboldt at front center, with the LSU Cadet Band.
(*Gumbo* 1934)

with the band and the attention and energy he devoted to it cannot be fully comprehended and may prove to be as complex and perplexing as the nature of the man himself. But one thing is certain: Long's influence sparked and then sustained the LSU Band's amazing metamorphosis and became the foundation of its first golden age.

FROM MILITARY TO SHOW BAND

At Long's request and insistence, Alfred W. Wickboldt (1874–1938) was appointed as LSU's band director in December 1930. According to T. Harry Williams's biography, *Huey Long,* the governor simply introduced Wickboldt to Commandant of Cadets Middleton in a terse conversation. Long explained that Wickboldt was a former army musician and bandmaster whom "someone" had told him about. With that comment, the conversation concluded, and Long and Wickboldt departed. With neither flourish nor fanfare, a new era in the band's history was ushered in.

Born and raised in Milwaukee, Wisconsin, Wickboldt studied music at the Milwaukee Conservatory of Music. Although he never completed a college degree, Wickboldt developed into an accomplished musician and became a featured trombone soloist with the Brookes Band and the Welden Band. From 1908 to 1930, he performed with the Emile E. Tosso Concert Orchestra and with the Orpheum Theater orchestra, both in New Orleans. During the Spanish-American War, Wickboldt served as chief musician and bandmaster of the 2nd United States Volunteer Infantry.

No one actually knows who brought Wickboldt to Long's attention, but it seems he knew relatively little of the musician and acted on impulse in hiring Wickboldt. Within two years of his appointment, the band had grown to a membership of 100, and it steadily increased in size. Wickboldt organized a drum and bugle corps to march and play as a unit of the Cadet Band, with the approval and backing of Long, whose election to the U.S. Senate had done nothing to diminish his involvement with the band. Comprised of twenty-four members, the Drum and Bugle Corps was equipped with twelve newly purchased snare drums and twelve bugles. This addition to the band brought its total membership to 125, making it by far the largest band in the university's history.

As promised, Long provided funding for new band uniforms, and he played an active role in designing the style and selecting the colors. Abandoning its long military tradition, the band was now clad in LSU's school colors: purple and gold. The flashy new uniforms signaled that the band was marching to a new drumbeat and in a new direction. Wickboldt thanked Long in 1931 by composing a new tune for the band, "The Governor Long March."

TRAVELS

The Cadet Band began to travel extensively. It crisscrossed Louisiana from Shreveport in the north to New Orleans in the south. Its road schedule took the band to Texas and as far away as New York. Long often accompanied the band and provided meal money for the musicians. In October 1931, the band traveled to Houston to perform at the LSU-Rice football game. Early in the day and prior to game time, with Long leading the way, the Cadet Band paraded through the streets of downtown Houston, to the delight—and perhaps amazement—of thousands of onlookers. Long took every opportunity to play the role of drum major. It was later reported that the Kingfish stole the show. The 1933 *Gumbo* reflected on another Houston trip in 1932: "It was a great day in Houston when the 150 cadets all clad in purple and gold stepped off the train and fell in behind Huey and his new white flannels and marched through the city to the rhythm of his walking cane that outdid the inimitable [drum major] Lew Williams and his whirling baton."

In November 1931, the LSU Cadet Band accompanied the football team to West Point, New York, for a game with the cadets of the United States Military Academy. Long, who engineered the trip, intended for the band to inspire the Tigers and to mesmerize the "crowd of Yankees" attending the game. The *New York Times* announced on November 6, 1931, that a special train of Louisiana supporters, accompanying a band

Huey Long watches "his" band. The location and date are unknown, but the photograph was produced by the Roumain Building Fine Arts Studio, Baton Rouge. (RBL)

The Cadet Band follows the parade of cadets in 1933 on the field of the new campus stadium. (DM3)

of 125 pieces, was due to arrive the next morning. At the game, the LSU Cadet Band was accorded a rare honor. The Academy's commandant of cadets requested that the band play West Point's alma mater at halftime.

SHOW BAND OF THE SOUTH

As the Cadet Band gained acclaim, it became known as the "Show Band of the South." Talented, entertaining drum majors led the LSU Show Band. Llewellyn Williams, named All-American Drum Major in 1931, made a striking appearance at six feet, four inches; including the height of his shako, he stood over seven feet tall. His successor, Burns Bennett, joined the band in 1934. On September 25, 1937, Steve Borne debuted at the head of the LSU Band. An admirer of Lew's and a two-time national high school champion drum major, Steve not only could twirl three batons at the same time, but also had a secret weapon: his brother Irvin, who joined in leading the Tiger Band. Steve left school in his sophomore year to become a professional educator, first teaching in

Vicksburg, Mississippi, and then in Chicago. He became one of LSU's World War II casualties when his plane went missing in the Southwest Pacific on November 21, 1944.[1]

Sometimes the Cadet Band had somber duties. It was only fitting that the band be present in November 1932 at the burial of LSU president Thomas Boyd, for Boyd had supported the band since its inception in 1893. The service was held at St. James Episcopal Church, where the church's organist, former LSU band director and Boyd's longtime friend W. B. Clarke, played hymns. When the cortege reached the corner of Dufrocq and Laurel Streets outside Magnolia Cemetery, the entire cadet corps met it. Led by the silent, instrumentless band, the corps moved before the coffin to the spot where Boyd was laid to rest. Frank T. Guilbeau, a friend of Boyd's for fifty years and former LSU bugler and band director, sounded taps.[2]

Drum major Irvin Borne leading the Cadet Band. (LSUPC)

WICKBOLDT DISMISSED

From all accounts, Wickboldt succeeded beyond expectation in transforming the LSU Band into the kind of organization Long had envisioned. The band had dramatically increased in size to become one of the largest university bands in America. The quality of its musical performance had greatly improved. It was now superbly equipped and uniformed. To Long's delight, it brought credit to LSU, to Louisiana, and to Long as well, whenever and wherever it performed. Apparently, however, all this was not enough. Without providing a reason and without a hearing, in December 1934 Long ordered LSU president James Monroe Smith to "retire" Wickboldt immediately. He then informed Smith that Wickboldt's successor had already been hired. The new band director's name was Castro Carazo.

THE AMAZING COLLABORATION: HUEY AND CASTRO

Born in Costa Rica, Castro Carazo (1895–1981) was educated at San José's Santa Cecilia School of Music, studying piano, violin, and music composition. He pursued advanced study in music composition and orchestration at the prestigious Barcelona Conservatory of Music in Spain. Carazo toured with a number of musical organizations and eventually served as leader of a small orchestra in one of the hundreds of dance clubs in New York City. He was responsible for rehearsing and conducting the orchestra and for creating special arrangements of popular dance tunes for it. Around

1922 he became music director at the Strand Theater in New Orleans, owned by the Saenger Amusement Company. When the Saenger Theatre opened in 1927, the company named Carazo music director. The Saenger was the foremost theater and music palace in New Orleans. Initially its movie menu included a broad array of silent films, and for these, Carazo composed and arranged musical scores as background music. The orchestra also entertained audiences before and between movies, quickly gaining popular acclaim. Theater patrons often remarked that they visited the Saenger as much to hear the orchestra and watch Carazo conduct as to enjoy the films.

About 1932, Carazo moved home to Costa Rica, where he was appointed general director of military bands for the government. But he soon returned to New Orleans as music director of the Roosevelt Hotel's Blue Room Orchestra, a post he held until his appointment as LSU's band director in December 1934. Locals recognized the Blue Room as the city's premier setting for dancing, imbibing, and relaxing. Because of its décor, large dance floor, and superb orchestra, wealthy New Orleanians flocked there.

FRIENDSHIP BEGINS

Long maintained a suite of rooms at the Roosevelt Hotel. The governor used his suite, as well as the Blue Room lounge, to entertain friends and associates and, quite often, to woo his political opposition—even to transact state business. As a frequent patron of the Blue Room, Long became acquainted with Carazo soon after he took over the orchestra in 1932. Long's initial attraction to the musician stemmed from their common love of music. Castro's Blue Room orchestra built a broad repertory of popular songs and dance tunes, many of which stylistically favored the romantic and nostalgic— precisely the kind of musical fare Long preferred.

When visiting the Blue Room, Long would sit with friends at a table near the bandstand and during intermissions invite Carazo to his table, engaging him in animated conversation. Blue Room guests commonly made requests for the orchestra to play their favorite songs. Eventually Long asked if the orchestra could play "Smoke Gets in Your Eyes," one of his favorite tunes. Castro obliged, and soon Long made numerous requests. In time, when Long would ask for a particular favorite, Carazo would invite him to take the director's baton and lead the orchestra. Eyewitnesses commented that Long always seemed delighted to do so and conducted the orchestra with enthusiasm and childlike glee. Although Long knew little about conducting, the orchestra never missed a beat.

CARAZO BECOMES BAND DIRECTOR

Tales abound surrounding Carazo's hiring as band director. Most of these share some elements of truth—and an intriguing mix of fact and fiction. One often-repeated story is that Long simply informed Carazo one night at the Blue Room that he was to be LSU's next bandmaster. The two men, along with Long's bodyguard and chauffeur, drove to Baton Rouge, where Carazo was ushered to Long's suite at the Heidelberg Hotel. He

Director Castro Carazo, in white suit at center, stands with the newer, larger band in 1935. (*Gumbo* 1935)

was told to telephone LSU president Smith and Commandant of Cadets Middleton and to inform them that Long wanted to meet with them at Governor O. K. Allen's office immediately. In the meeting, Long simply announced that he had hired Carazo to fill the band director's position, and stipulated that Carazo was to answer to himself, Smith, and Middleton, and to no one else. Long authorized Smith and Middleton to provide Carazo with anything and everything he required to transform the LSU Band into the nation's largest and best; he would always find the money. With that, Long abruptly closed the meeting. Soon after Carazo's appointment, Governor Allen authorized a commission for Carazo as a "colonel" of his staff. Although it was an honorific rank, from that time on he was addressed as Colonel Carazo.[3]

The 1940 band. (*Gumbo* 1940)

Upon assuming control of the band, Carazo began to reorganize as outlined by Long. To increase the band's membership, he developed a plan for recruiting new student musicians. He offered scholarships, with Long providing the necessary funding, to all who joined the band. The ability to play an instrument well was not always a firm prerequisite. Carazo's ultimate goal in terms of student enrollment was to expand the organization to 250 musicians, complying with Long's demand that LSU have the largest college band in America.

A larger band needed more instruments than were available in the band's inventory. With Long's approval and support, the influx of new instruments kept pace with the band's rapid growth. Within two school years, the inventory satisfied the instrumental needs of a 200-member band. Carazo did not neglect the band's music library, filling it with music of every genre. A superb musician himself, he built a comprehensive and balanced band music collection that more than adequately met both concert and marching needs. By the end of his five-year tenure, the music library rivaled in size and scope that of any university in the South. Until destroyed in the 1958 Band House fire, it was one of the most complete university band libraries in America.

Carazo's next priority was the acquisition of new band uniforms. Long's hand in designing the uniform was clear and unmistakable, resulting in a more colorful, flashier style than any the band had ever worn. The new uniforms included trousers, coat, and hat, all in LSU purple and ornamented in gold, with wide gold stripes extending vertically down the outside seams of the trousers. Under the coat, each cadet wore a long-sleeve white dress shirt with a purple or gold tie. A second pair of trousers in white gave the band a different look. To Long's delight, the dazzling new uniforms dramatized a clear shift from military band to show band.

CARAZO'S MUSIC

In his first year as band director, Carazo began composing songs and other pieces for the university. He wrote a stirring march, "The LSU Cadets," which he dedicated to the Corps of Cadets. "Darling of LSU" and "Touchdown for LSU" quickly followed, both of them products of a unique collaboration with Long. Typically, Long wrote words of a song that had "just come to him," telephoned Carazo, and regardless of the hour of the day or night, instructed the band director to meet with him immediately. He presented Carazo with a sheet of crumpled paper on which he had scribbled lyrics that he expected Carazo to set to music. Hours would pass with Carazo at the piano and Long nervously pacing the floor as music and words slowly began to flow together. Their unlikely teamwork produced songs that quickly became popular on campus and beyond. "Touchdown for LSU" is heard today at all home football games as the Tiger Band marches downfield in its formal pregame entrance. As the team leaves its dressing room and rushes onto the field through a human tunnel formed by the Tiger Band, it does so to the rousing strains of Carazo's 1937 "Fight for LSU." That piece sparked spontaneous popularity and eventually became LSU's official fight song. After more than seventy-five years, the two fight songs Carazo composed are still popular today and are tightly woven into the fabric of LSU's history and tradition.

One other musical collaboration between Long and Carazo is noteworthy. Together, they produced a very special song that has come to be intimately associated with the myths and legends of the enigmatic politician. This unforgettable piece, the nostalgic "Every Man a King," became Long's campaign song. When Long was assassinated in November of 1935, Carazo composed a funeral dirge with threads of "Every Man a King" embedded within the strains. The LSU Band played it then as Carazo's farewell and musical tribute to the friend he had come to love and respect.

THE BAND HOUSE

By 1932, the band had outgrown the Practice House. Rehearsals moved to LSU's gym armory, which proved to be inconvenient and inadequate. At Carazo's urging, the university administration authorized an expansion of the Practice House. The addition consisted of a large rehearsal hall, a cedar-lined uniform storage room, a music library, an instrument repair laboratory, instrument storage space, and offices for the band director and the band's secretary. Coupled with the existing structure, the new construction created a band complex with two rehearsal halls and sufficient space to satisfy the organization's physical needs for the next two decades. The cadet musicians quickly renamed their new home the "Band House," but it is most often referred to as simply the band hall.

ADDED ATTRACTIONS

In large part, Carazo's success as orchestra leader at the Saenger Theatre and later at the Roosevelt Hotel Blue Room can be attributed to his ability to entertain and enthrall audiences. He never lost his gift of showmanship and certainly brought it with him to LSU, where he organized a female twirling and dance squad to perform with the marching band. Never before had women been included in any capacity in the all-male organization. Carazo aptly named the new unit the "Tigerettes." He intended that they would add more glitz to the emerging Show Band, thus enhancing its audience appeal.

Two of the Tigerettes, sisters Juliette and Marie Louise Bonnette, who became known as the "Dancing Darlings of LSU," also performed with the cheerleading squad. Carazo capitalized on their campus fame and showcased them in twirling and dance routines with the band as it performed. When interviewed by the *Register* (a magazine focusing on Baton Rouge's social scene) in 1968, they recalled that news reporters came up with ideas for their photographs, such as placing the sisters on giant pigs at the agricultural shows and staging them dancing on ledges and the back of trucks, as well as having the drum major brothers, the Bornes, twirl heavy batons over their heads.[4]

Plans for the band's reorganization included reconstituting the Drum and Bugle Corps as a unit within the band. Carazo increased its size from the original twenty-four

Words and music to two of LSU's most acclaimed songs, written by Huey P. Long and Castro Carazo and printed in 1935. (Louisiana Collection, LLMVC)

top left: Juliette and Marie Louise Bonnette, the "Dancing Darlings of LSU," seated on the sugar kettle on the LSU campus in 1936. Standing is Michael Grace. (Photograph courtesy of Mike Nelson)

top right: Castro used the Bonnette sisters in many new productions for the band. (Photograph by Fonville Winans, courtesy of Mike Nelson. Used with the permission of Robert L. Winans.)

right: Castro also made greater use of the Purple Jackets in band routines. (*Gumbo* 1940)

members to forty. Cadets of the Drum and Bugle Corps wore the same uniforms as the band when they marched and performed with it. At times, however, the corps operated independently, providing music for ROTC revues and parades. When it did so, the unit dressed in the military uniform of the cadet corps.

Carazo's final addition to the marching band was the "Purple Jackets." Comprised of seventy female students, the group had been established in 1933 as a university-sponsored service organization. When they performed with the band, the Purple Jackets dressed in white shoes and socks, white skirts, white long-sleeve blouses, gold neck scarves, waist-length purple jackets, and white army-style caps. In addition to functioning as one of the band's auxiliary units, the Purple Jackets regularly participated in a variety of campus events, including rallies, convocations, and official ceremonies of the university.

PUBLICIZING THE BAND

Carazo understood the value of positive publicity. In 1936, without first seeking approval of the university administration, he organized the band's own public relations department, interviewing and hiring three journalism students to record and photograph the activities of the band and its related units. The student publicists quickly established contacts with news reporters of local and distant media outlets, barraging them with information on all the accomplishments of the band and its leader. For a time, the public relations department flourished, but to Carazo's surprise, the band's burgeoning notoriety became a source of resentment in several university departments, especially the military. The ROTC complained to the university administration of the band's "dangerously increasing prominence" as a campus organization. Carazo's fledgling creation was abruptly terminated.

At the close of Carazo's second year as director, the LSU Band was recognized for the quality of its performances wherever it appeared. It steadily continued to evolve into the show band of Huey Long's dreams. The *Beaumont (TX) Enterprise* reported in September 1936: "Along with others, doubtless, we often wondered what intense attraction LSU, particularly the LSU Band, held for Huey Long. Saturday we divined a reason. The Tiger band is one of the best. In fact, we doubt that we have ever seen a better one. It is big, talented, well drilled and snappy. If this writer could have felt that he wouldn't have been pushed on his face he would have got out there himself and done a little strutting. That band is a pip."

CARAZO'S TRAVELS

From his earliest days as governor, Huey Long was not averse to using the LSU Band to focus public attention on himself. Llewellyn Williams Jr., the high-stepping former LSU drum major who marched side by side with Long in parades and at football

Drum major Burns Bennett looks on while "Every Man a King" is played one last time for Huey Long as his coffin leaves the Louisiana State Capitol in September 1935. (Charles East Papers, Mss. 3471, LLMVC)

games from 1929 to 1933, recalled that "Huey liked to parade with the band. He was always over on the right hand side just having a ball, dressed in a white suit and a white hat. He loved the ballyhoo." Long helped Williams attend LSU, and they remained friends until Long's death.[5]

Long also regarded the band as a vehicle for promoting LSU and Louisiana. The band, therefore, would not remain "hidden" at home but would travel throughout the state and far beyond its borders. And travel it certainly did! It is probable that in the five years of Carazo's tenure, the band logged more miles by bus and train than any other university band in America. By the late 1930s, the band's popularity with the general public had reached its zenith. It was common for fans attending an LSU football game to comment that they had come to see the band as much as to enjoy the game itself.

Many of the band's accomplishments can be traced directly to Long's support, but it was Carazo who, by virtue of his personality, leadership, musicianship, and creativity, had transformed the band into the magnificent organization it had become. Long and Carazo shared far more than their love of music. Both men were blessed with great intelligence; both possessed strong, perhaps overpowering personalities; both were highly creative; both were flamboyant; both had a strong flair for showmanship; both were controversial; and both were gifted leaders. It is not surprising that they developed a strong and lasting relationship from which emerged a unique collaboration. After Long's assassination in 1935, a drastic change occurred in Carazo's career and life—and in the leadership of the LSU Band.

CARAZO'S TIME ENDS

The next two governors after Huey Long, Oscar Allen and Richard W. Leche, were former members of Long's inner circle. Despite the influx of generous amounts of money from the federal government for Works Progress Administration projects in the state, Leche was forced to resign in June 1939. Handpicked by Long in 1931, Smith continued as president of LSU until he was also forced to resign in June 1939. Smith was convicted of embezzling university funds; Leche was convicted of, among other charges, diverting federal money for private use and misusing LSU funds. Both went to prison.

A new reform governor, Sam H. Jones, took office in May 1940. Jones appointed his own people to the LSU Board of Supervisors and sought to erase Longism from the LSU campus. Many people formerly associated with Long were fired. In spite of accolades from every quarter, on August 23, 1940, Carazo was summarily dismissed as the university's band director. Frank Wickes, LSU's longest-serving band director (1980–2010), offers this tribute: "Although Senator Long's assassination in the fall of 1935 would cut short his budding love affair with the LSU Band, Castro Carazo's efforts as influenced by Long continued throughout the 1930s. Thanks to the impeccable style and musicality of Carazo, the band enjoyed a period of unmatched evolution and fame."[6]

A Jones supporter, Major General Campbell B. Hodges, became LSU's new president. The songs written by Carazo and Long were forbidden by Hodges to be played by the band. Military gray uniforms replaced the flashy gold and purple loved by Carazo and Long, reflecting the new, somber tone. Faculty in the School of Music took over supervision of all band activities, except those of the auxiliary Drum and Bugle Corps. On February 13, 1941, the director of the School of Music announced that the name of the band would no longer be the LSU Cadet Band but the LSU Band.[7]

Because of the intensifying war in Europe, the American military was also changing. After the United States entered World War II, cadets on the LSU campus were discouraged from participating in campus activities, including the band. By October 1943, Hodges made a significant change. In a memo to the university comptroller, Hodges stated that the LSU Band had been placed entirely under control of the School of Music, the director of which would be responsible for all expenditures related to the band and for supervising band directors. It was truly no longer the Cadet Band.[8]

With the metamorphosis from military to show band accomplished, the LSU Band's first golden age came to a close. In the coming decades, two more would follow.

In the 1920s and 1930s, Jasper Ewing was one of the best-known Baton Rouge photographers who dared taking photographs from a small airplane. His aerial of "Gov. Leche" spelled by the LSU Band was taken in 1936. (Jasper Ewing and Sons, Photographs and Papers, Mss. 3141, LLMVC)

A contrasting aerial to that of Ewing's shows the Tiger Band in the famous "LSU" formation in a stadium more than twice as large as the one in 1936. (LSU Band)

The "LSU" formation from near ground level at the 2005 national championship game.
(Photograph by Rachel Saltzberg)

Raymond Joseph Borne served as the LSU Band drum major as did his cousins Steve and Irvin Borne. Raymond served before he joined the military in World War II, 1943. (Photograph courtesy of Linda Saucier)

3

THE WAR YEARS
1941–1945

When the war came, everything changed. Its impact was profound, affecting every person and every institution in America. LSU and its band were no exceptions. In World War II, LSU was ranked with the Military Academy, the Naval Academy, and Texas A&M as the top four universities to provide college-trained manpower for the armed forces. Twelve thousand former LSU students answered the call to military service. Among them were five thousand who achieved officer rank and sixteen who rose to the rank of general. Of the LSU alumni who fought on every front, more than five hundred never came home.

A. Manly Culpepper and James S. Fisher. (LSU Band)

BEFORE THE STORM

On August 28, 1940, just five days after Carazo's dismissal, Arthur Manly Culpepper (1891–1954) was named as acting band director. Nine years earlier, he had joined the faculty of the LSU School of Music, although he had not yet earned a college diploma. His responsibilities included teaching undergraduate classes in music theory and music history, and leading the university's intramural music program. While a full-time member of the faculty, he earned two degrees from LSU, the bachelor of music in 1934 and the master of music in 1938. Culpepper's appointment as permanent director was approved in February 1941.[1] Immediately upon his appointment, Culpepper selected James S. Fisher (b. ca. 1915), former music director at the Louisiana State School for the Blind, as his assistant band director.

To become acquainted with the bandsmen and to prepare them for the 1940 football season, Culpepper and Fisher notified the members to report for rehearsal three days prior to the start of regular classes. Approximately two hundred student musicians responded, including members of the independent auxiliary Drum and Bugle Corps. With the approval of the Military Department, the ranks of the marching band absorbed members of the Drum and Bugle Corps. Consequently, the organization was officially disbanded as an independent auxiliary unit of the band.

Those first rehearsals focused on the rudiments of marching, block-band precision drill, and music performance. The directors knew that the band's success on the gridiron would be determined by the extent of each bandsman's mastery of these basic fundamentals. In 1940, like most other university bands, the LSU band's halftime performances were comprised of a mix of precision drill and "pageantry," a general term used to describe formations on the field of letters, words, and simple pictures. In organizing the band's halftime performances, Culpepper and Fisher had to plot and chart each marcher's actions. Music appropriate to the band's precision drills and formations required perfect coordination with the bandsmen's movements. Finally, halftime performances had to be timed and synchronized to fit the twelve-minute time frames allotted to them. Spectators knew little of the planning and rehearsals that occurred behind the scenes before each performance. With so little time to prepare for the 1940 season's opening game, LSU's new band directors had their work cut out for them.[2]

Culpepper and Fisher recognized the challenge they faced in assuming leadership of LSU's acclaimed marching band. Only weeks before the first football game and the band's first performance of the 1940 school year, they had accepted the responsibility of maintaining the quality of the organization and of upholding its reputation as one of the largest and best university bands in America. Working together, the director and his assistant produced a band almost as large as its recent predecessors and one that marched and played extremely well, but something intangible was missing. The band no longer reflected the showmanship that had been second nature to its former director, Castro Carazo. Gone were the glitz and glitter of LSU's colorful show bands that in the past had thrilled spectators in Tiger Stadium and around the country.[3]

Despite the lack of Carazo-style performances, the Tiger Band maintained a remarkably busy schedule. According to the LSU student newspaper the *Reveille,* when Culpepper read an editorial in the *Minnesota Daily* saying that the University of Minnesota band made more public appearances than any other university band except Illinois, "it made his spring fever rise."[4] Culpepper boasted that the LSU Tiger Band was a rival to both the Minnesota and Illinois bands, and its activities proved so. During the fall 1941 semester, the Tiger Band provided music for two freshman-week convocations and prepared for nine upcoming football game shows. In addition to a New Orleans trip for the Tulane game, the band played for the Harding Field air base dedication and Armistice Day parade and ceremonies. During the 1942 spring semester, most members of the marching band also joined the Concert Band, which played weekly programs for the community.

NOTHING REMAINS THE SAME

With four wins, four losses, and two ties, the Tiger football team's 1941 season was less than stellar. There was, however, one bright spot in an otherwise dismal season: in the final game, on November 29, 1941, the LSU Tigers emerged victorious over archrival Tulane by a score of 19–0. This win over the Green Wave would not in itself be remarkable, much less memorable, except for one thing. Just eight days later, the Japanese bombed Pearl Harbor, the United States declared war, and the world changed.[5]

On January 16, 1942, sixty-five students resigned from LSU to volunteer for military service. Soon a flood of students and faculty followed, while others were called up in the nationwide draft. As a result, the university's enrollment tumbled from a high of seven thousand in 1938 to three thousand by late 1942. To satisfy wartime demands for college-trained manpower in June 1942, LSU, like other schools across the country, developed accelerated programs as they had done during World War I. These made it possible for students to graduate in three years rather than four and improved the chances of males graduating before being drafted into military service, thus providing the military with a steady flow of trained professionals. With the departure of so many young men, for the first time in LSU's history enrollment of females exceeded that of males.[6] Reflecting universitywide trends, the band's membership also declined.

On July 1, 1942, Culpepper resigned his position as LSU's band director to return to the U.S. Army Air Corps in which he had served during World War I. In World War II, he

On the parade ground in front of the LSU Tower, 1941. (*Gumbo* 1941)

Fisher and the Concert Band on stage. The women musicians also served in the marching band. (Photograph courtesy of Linda Saucier)

was a commanding officer of a division of the Air Service Mechanics Training School at Kelly Field, Texas. His tenure as director had lasted slightly less than two years.[7]

WOMEN MUSICIANS

Women had never been permitted to join the band as student musicians. But at the midpoint of the war, the loss of so many young men to military service left the band's ranks severely depleted. The only viable solution to its shrinking enrollment meant abandoning one of LSU's time-honored traditions. In September 1942, Fisher, who had been appointed band director after Culpepper's departure, received permission from university administrators to form an "all-girl band" for the "benefit of girls' musical education" and to fill spaces in the all-male Concert Band. It was reluctantly decided that the time had also come to admit women to full participation in the marching band. For the first time in its half-century existence and out of wartime necessity, women were integrated into the band as musicians.

At a band practice in 1944, drum major Woodrow W. Blalock realized that other than band director Fisher, he was the only male present. Although only nineteen years old, and confused and frightened about the war, "I decided then and there I was in the wrong place, resigned and joined the Army Air Corps," said Blalock in 1990. Raymond

Joseph Borne served as the next drum major until he enlisted in the service in 1943; he returned as drum major at the end of the war. Raymond was a cousin of Steve and Irvin Borne, who had been drum majors in the Carazo-era band. Evelyn Delery Duncan wanted to join the band when she arrived at LSU in 1942 but realized it might not ever be possible. She recalled, "They didn't call girls into the band until 1943 to hold the band together because all the men were off to war." Evelyn performed as one of the two drum majorettes. It took some time for the university administration to become accustomed to giving women band scholarships, however. In the spring semester of 1944, the director of the School of Music had to remind LSU's president that "Miss Marie Burt and Miss Regina Champagne are regular members of the LSU band and should get their registration fees returned."[8]

Violet Blackwood Lux, who played the bassoon and flute, was among the first women officially added to the band roster. She recalled in 1986 that there were six or seven female members in 1943. "We had to wear the men's uniforms, tuck our hair up in the cap, wear no makeup and even wear men's shoes."[9] In the 1940s, however, it was generally considered inappropriate for young ladies of college age to dress in pants or slacks. Since women were now expected to march alongside the male bandsmen and within the band's ranks, it became necessary to provide uniforms of white, pleated skirts in place of the traditional purple pants. Otherwise, their uniforms would be identical to those of the men. Dot Brammer and Janet Steele also joined the band in 1943. Janet married Raymond Borne when he returned after war service to resume his role as drum major.

As early as 1936, the band's uniform had included two pairs of trousers, one purple and one white. In those peacetime years, white pants provided a bit of relief and vari-

left: Dot Brammer and Janet Steele were among the first female band members. Here they are shown in uniforms that match the men's, 1946. (Photograph courtesy of Linda Saucier)

right: Female drum majorettes Betty Ellendar and Evelyn Delery. (*Gumbo* 1944)

Raymond Borne returned from military service and again became the band's drum major in 1945. (Photograph courtesy of Linda Saucier)

ation from the more formal all-purple attire. Beginning in early 1942, white trousers were mandated out of necessity. Funding problems and wartime shortages combined to make it impossible to replace the band's purple uniforms. To protect them from undue wear and tear, the complete ensemble of trousers, coat, and hat was reserved exclusively for the band's concert and football performances. For all other appearances, including military revues and parades, white trousers were substituted for the purple ones, or the band wore cadet gray. In 1943, with the newly inducted females wearing white skirts and the male bandsmen dressed in white pants, the band's overall appearance was less drab and in fact improved remarkably. For many of its performances spanning the remainder of the war, the LSU Band was attired in white bottoms and purple tops.

BAND DIRECTORS

After Culpepper's resignation in 1942, three other men served as LSU's band director in the remaining years of the war. This rapid turnover in leadership was unprecedented in the band's history. Fisher, Culpepper's assistant, was promoted to director in July 1942. He had received a bachelor of music in 1935 and a master in music in 1939, both from LSU. After eighteen months, Fisher resigned and enlisted in the U.S. Marine Corps. At the time of his departure from LSU on January 21, 1944, the band's enrollment numbered fewer than eighty student musicians.

Fisher was followed by William E. Koogler (1915–1965), a School of Music faculty member who was named acting director. Koogler earned a performer's certificate in clarinet from Ohio State University and a bachelor of music degree from the Eastman School of Music. Before coming to LSU, he served as assistant director of band and orchestra at the University of Arizona. On October 1, 1944, Koogler was relieved as band director. He returned to teaching duties in the School of Music and resigned from LSU in January 1945. His brief tenure lasted for only nine months.[10]

Membership in the band, even with female participation, had fallen to a wartime low of fifty-four. Perhaps as testament of the times, LSU's next and last wartime band director was a senior in the School of Music. In October 1944, Andrew J. McMullen (b. ca. 1925) was named interim director and served until September 1945. Not since the band's founding in 1893, when a future governor was chosen by his fellow cadets to lead the university's first band, had a student held that position. Much to his credit, McMullen managed to guide the band through the remainder of the 1944 football season and, remarkably, was able to avoid a collapse of the war-depleted organization. On May 9, 1945, McMullen and some members of the LSU Band even served as the "honor band" of the day for the inauguration parade of Governor-elect James Davis.[11]

With the war concluded and a slow but steady return to more normal times, the LSU Band experienced a rebirth. Under new, energetic leadership, the band's former place on the national stage would in time be restored.

BAND AWARDS BANQUET

May 21, 1946

OFFICERS

Leslie Gautreau . . . . . President

Raymond Borne . . . Vice-President

Dorothy Riggins . . . . . Secretary

Louis Mattison . . . . . Treasurer

Jay Jalenak . . . . . . Publicity

PROGRAM

Dr. Barrett Stout, Toastmaster

Invocation . . . . . Harry Rounsaville

Quartette . . Hugo Morara, David Johnson
Bill Pruyn, Vernon Taranto

Showing of Football Pictures

Recordings of Spring Concert

Presentation of Band Awards. L. Bruce Jones

Special Music . . . . . . Quartette

Speaker . . . . Dean Fred C. Frey

Alma Mater

Program for the 1946 band awards banquet. The poor-quality mimeograph is indicative of the band's postwar financial struggles. (Program courtesy of Linda Saucier)

The Golden Band from Tigerland performs at a Saints game. (LSU Band)

Drums on the field, 2010. (Photograph by Rachel Saltzberg)

L. Bruce Jones, LSU's first post–World War II band director. (*Gumbo* 1952)

Thomas Tyra, who became director of marching bands in August 1958. (LSU Band)

4

A TALE OF
TWO DIRECTORS
1946–1964

Four years of war left LSU intact but drastically changed. Enrollment had declined by half; enlistments and the draft had decimated the faculty; diverse courses of study had been terminated; some sports programs, including football, had been curtailed while others were eliminated altogether; and campus buildings had fallen into varying states of disrepair because of deferred maintenance. The LSU of 1945 was a very different university from the LSU of prewar days. The state of its band mirrored the circumstances surrounding the university. Year by year, membership had declined steadily, from a high of two hundred in 1940 to a low of fifty-four in 1944. The band's inventory of musical instruments was depleted because those beyond repair could not be replaced. The traditional uniforms of purple and gold were threadbare and no longer usable. Needed repairs on the Band House were neglected. Fortunately, LSU's administrators were determined to reorganize and rebuild the school's once-renowned marching band. They understood that success would depend on finding a director with proven ability, practical experience, and strong credentials. L. Bruce Jones proved to be a perfect fit for the position. To revive the band, however, would require the talents of two men. Spanning nineteen years, the combined successes of directors L. Bruce Jones and Tom Tyra transformed LSU's Tiger Band and restored its fame.

BAND HOUSE RENOVATION

Wartime priorities combined with scant resources led to a serious deterioration of the condition of the Band House. During the war years, the dilapidated rehearsal facility received little attention other than some painting and general carpentry. The time had come to renovate the building, and contracts were awarded for its remodeling. With the promise of GI Bill money and more students, in late 1945 LSU's administration also approved funding to repair and recondition the band's instruments and to replace those beyond further use. The Band House renovation was completed just in time for the start of the fall semester. The administration then initiated an intensive search to identify and hire a person who could breathe new life into the band and restore it to the national stage.

L. BRUCE JONES

On September 1, 1945, Llewellyn Bruce Jones (1905–1976) was named LSU's first postwar band director. Jones held bachelor of science degrees from Northeast Missouri State Teachers College and the University of Illinois, as well as a master of arts in music education from Peabody Teachers' College. Since 1928 he had directed the award-winning band of Little Rock High School in Arkansas. Just seven years after Jones arrived, that band placed first in the annual national high school band competition. In 1942, it was selected to play a live concert on NBC radio's *Music and American Youth* series. Jones's professional reputation derived from the quality of the Little Rock organization plus his service as president of the National School Bands Association, on the board of directors of the American Bandmasters' Association, and on the editorial board of the *Music Educators' Journal.*

Soon after arriving at LSU in 1945, Jones selected David A. Ledet, his former assistant in Little Rock, as assistant band director. Ledet played oboe in the Little Rock

The Band House after renovation, as shown in the program for the LSU Concert Band, spring concert tour, May 1946. (Program courtesy of Linda Saucier)

High School Band and was its drum major for three years. With LSU's football season only weeks away and no experienced drum major in the Tiger Band's depleted ranks, Ledet agreed to serve in that capacity. He gained the distinction of becoming the first and only assistant director in the band's history to play that dual role. For the opening home game against Rice University and the Tiger Band's first halftime show since the war's end, Ledet marched onto the field followed by two men twirlers leading a hopeful new group of bandsmen.

A third staff member joined the Band Department in September 1946. Hired as instrument repairman and second assistant to Jones, James N. Geideman—"Mr. G.," as he came to be fondly called—would remain with the department until his retirement in 1976. During those three decades, Geideman earned the respect and admiration of all those fortunate enough to know him.

Jones nurtured the close association between the Tiger Band and the university's Purple Jackets, which had flourished over many years as they marched together in parades and performed together at home and away football games. To prepare the Purple Jackets for halftime performances with the band, Geideman served as their drill instructor. Working with the women apart from the musicians, he painstakingly taught them the rudiments of marching. Once they had mastered their part in the upcoming halftime show and were ready to rehearse with the band, the two organizations combined and practiced together. Mr. G.'s gentleness and thoroughness in working with the Purple Jackets always paid off.

In 1944, the Tiger Band's membership, including women, dipped to a wartime low of fifty-four musicians. With frantic recruiting, Jones and Ledet managed to scrape together a total of seventy in time for the first game of the 1945 football season. For the Tulane game in New Orleans on November 30, Jones fielded a contingent of almost ninety musicians and thirty-three Purple Jackets. Although their uniforms were dull khaki, except for the Purple Jackets' gold trim, the band staged an elaborate show.

James N. Geideman on his retirement day in 1976. (Photograph by Johnny Gordon)

GIs RETURN

By the following season of 1946, the band's enrollment crisis ended as thousands of veterans taking advantage of the GI Bill poured into the university. Scores of these new students, many trained in wartime military bands, joined the Tiger Band and swelled its membership to 120. This infusion of energy, talent, and maturity added immeasurably to the band's quality and ensured its speedy revival. In 1990, Esper K. Chandler, a bandsman from 1946 to 1949, recalled how tough those GI bandsmen were when they marched in pouring rain at the University of Alabama, although the Alabama band declined to do so. The year of rebuilding brought the band praise from the *LSU Alumni News,* which reported: "When the strutting, baton twirling drum major leads the Tiger Band onto the field at football games, the spectators cheer one of LSU's oldest organizations—the Band—as it greets the visiting school with intricate formations and spirited music.

Tigerettes raise money for a new Mike the Tiger, 1956. (OPRR)

The ability of the bandsmen to execute those formations without missing steps, bumbling for proper spacing, or indecision resulted from grinding practice and the able direction of bandmaster Jones."[1]

Under Jones's leadership, a newly created Band Department within the School of Music consisted of three organizations: the Concert, Varsity, and Tiger Bands. During football season, the two symphonic ensembles combined to form the Tiger Band. Freshman and sophomore ROTC cadets, if musically qualified, could also elect to play in the Tiger Band. On the recommendation of the ROTC director of student life, however, in October 1946, LSU president William B. Hatcher rescinded the prewar policy of excusing students who registered for band from military service. Nonmilitary personnel in nonmilitary attire could not legally march with the cadets. Therefore, a military band comprised of men fulfilling their military requirements was created. Control and management of the ROTC Band resided with the commandant of cadets and the Military Department. An arrangement between the latter and the School of Music designated Jones as director of the ROTC Band. The ROTC Band provided music for all martial reviews and dress parades. Participants could also audition for membership in the Tiger Band. According to a 1949 bulletin, the Band Department was composed of eight units: the Concert and Varsity Bands, whose members presented concerts on campus and in the community and went on yearly tours; two marching bands, the Tiger Band for football games and a military band for ROTC events; and four pep bands, whose members came from the Tiger Band. According to the bulletin, the Beta Gamma chapter of Kappa Kappa Psi, the national band honorary society, was chartered in 1948.[2]

PARADING TIGER BAND

Before World War II, the Tiger Band had marched throughout the state in a variety of parades, but it could not accept all the invitations it received. Some invitations conflicted with students' classes during football season, or with other events in the spring when the Tiger Band was divided into the symphonic bands. When a strong, impressive Tiger Band reemerged at the end of 1945, requests for off-campus appearances resumed. For example, in February 1946, representatives of the School of Design, which staged the annual Rex parade in New Orleans on Mardi Gras, invited the band to march. University dean Fred Frey declined the request because the band was scheduled to appear at Armed Forces Day events on campus that day. The Rex organization was unhappy with the dean's response.

Throughout the history of the Tiger Band, the struggle for balance between campus and class obligations of the student members and demands for participation from various outside organizations was a source of conflict. However, the band always marched in Louisiana governors' inaugural parades. An old friend joined them for Governor Earl Long's inaugural on May 12, 1948. After the parade through Baton Rouge streets ended at the LSU stadium, Castro Carazo led the Southeastern Louisiana College Band in a

The Tiger Band leads a parade celebrating the arrival of Mike II. (OPRR)

concert. In 1952 the parade for Governor Robert Kennon ended at the State Capitol, where the LSU Band along with the Southwestern Louisiana Industrial Institute Band gave a concert. LSU's ROTC Band had paraded directly behind the governor's official car.

In the 1950s, there were special school events such as leading the parade celebrating the arrival of a new Mike the Tiger.

top: The Tiger Band forms a medical syringe on the field to encourage students to get flu shots. (*Gumbo* 1961)

bottom: New, unique formations included cannon. (*Gumbo* 1964)

HALFTIME INNOVATIONS

In fall 1948, working closely with Houston C. Jenks, the recently hired assistant band director, Jones reestablished the organization's reputation as one of America's finest college marching bands. The Tiger Band had successfully completed the transition from its wartime style of military marching back to the more colorful show band format of halftime entertainment introduced by Carazo. Under Jones's direction, the Tiger Band became known for the power and beauty of its music and for its machinelike precision on the gridiron. In collaboration, Jones and Jenks devised a series of innovations that elevated the band's halftime performances beyond any ever seen in Tiger Stadium. The first of these was the introduction of musical interludes played by the bandsmen as they transitioned from one formation to another. Previously they marched in lockstep, moving between formations to the beat of drum cadences. These musical lulls in the show's thematic continuity became predictable, boring, and monotonous, causing spectators to lose interest. The solution Jones and Jenks found was simple, yet novel for the time. Music, thematically related to the formations, replaced the drum cadences. Thereafter, the bandsmen played not only while standing in formation, but also while moving from one formation to another. From the first note of the band's halftime performance to the last, the flow of music was never significantly interrupted.

Another innovation Jones and Jenks generated lifted the spectacle of halftime in Tiger Stadium to another height. Since the early 1930s, pageantry had evolved into a popular art form. Spectators at high school and college football games judged bands on the novelty of the pictures bandsmen outlined on the field. Generally a series of picture formations told a story or presented a special theme. With few exceptions, the formations were stationary—they did not move, nor did they have moving parts. Inevitably, the static display of pageantry lost its novelty. To avoid this from happening with the Tiger Band, Jones and Jenks designed formations that were not frozen in place, but moved up and down and across the field. Certain formations not only moved but also had moving parts. An outlined picture of a locomotive steamed down the field with wheels turning and puffs of white smoke pouring from its stack, accompanied by the strains of the band's rendition of "Chattanooga Choo-Choo" and the deafening sound of a train whistle blaring from the stadium's public address system. Precise mathematical calculations, intricate planning, and increased rehearsal time were required to perfect the moving sequences and bring the formations to life. The results justified the time and effort—spectators watched mesmerized and rewarded the band with standing ovations. In designing formations of such complexity and teaching the bandsmen to execute them flawlessly on the field, Jones and Jenks stretched the limits of gridiron pageantry to the extreme.

They also reintroduced the "Tigerettes," a women's twirling and dance squad first included and named by Carazo, to the marching band's performances. But perhaps the most spectacular of their innovations was the annual lights show. Conceived by Jenks and embraced by Jones, the show required almost two thousand hours to plan and rehearse. The final product lasted only about twelve minutes but was certainly something to see. To create the lights show, the bandsmen and Purple Jackets were issued pocket-size flashlights that attached to their hats. Each also received four tiny plastic caps of red, gold, green, and blue that could be fitted over the flashlight bulb. Including the bulb that shone white, the bandsmen and Purple Jackets had the option of using five different colors in outlining the show's many formations. When the band marched onto the field at halftime, the stadium lights were immediately darkened. Until the conclusion of the performance, only the brilliant colors streaming from the hats of the bandsmen and Purple Jackets lighted the formations. Invariably, the impact on the fans was stunning. Throughout the halftime performance, their cheers and applause drowned out the sound of the 120-member band.

Night game performance with the lights show. (LSU Band)

BAND HOUSE FIRE

The most grievous tragedy in all the band's history occurred in the early morning hours of March 19, 1958. The wood-framed Band House burned to the ground. Fortunately, the three students who roomed in the building and served as nighttime caretakers escaped uninjured. With the exception of a few instruments, however, everything was destroyed. Only the walls of the gutted building remained, and damage was estimated at more than one hundred thousand dollars. Physical losses included a complete set of new Tiger Band uniforms, the Concert Band's one hundred tuxedos, almost the entire inventory of instruments, all of the band's equipment, and the tools in the instrument repair shop.

Other losses suffered that morning were even more devastating. The photographs and historical records protected and preserved since the band's founding were lost. Gone too were the priceless recordings of band performances dating as far back as the late 1920s. Above all else of intrinsic value, the band's irreplaceable music library was reduced to ashes.

On September 1, 1958, within five months of the fire, Jones hired Thomas N. Tyra (1933–1995) as assistant director and director of marching bands (the Tiger Band and the ROTC Band). Less than one year later and after fourteen years of distinguished service to LSU, L. Bruce Jones resigned as band director but remained a professor of music education until his retirement in 1976. By any measure, his achievements at Little Rock High School and LSU merited the national recognition he received.

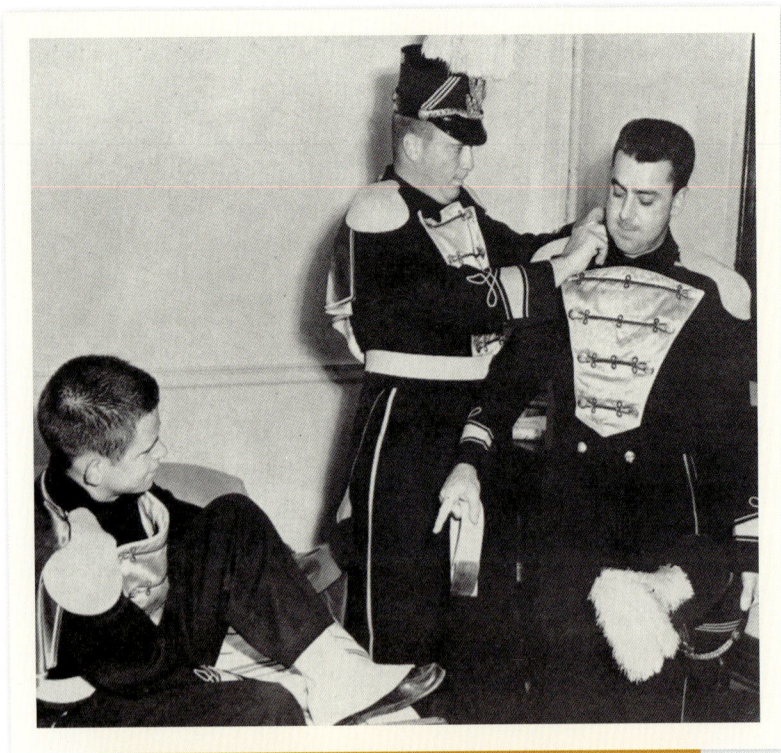

Bandsmen adjust their new uniforms. (*Gumbo* 1959)

THOMAS N. TYRA

Tyra was energetic, enthusiastic, creative, innovative, and charismatic—and he had a penchant for showmanship. Tyra attended Northwestern University in Evanston, Illinois. He completed a bachelor of music in education degree in 1954 and, one year later, the master of music in education. As a member of Northwestern's student band staff, Tyra assisted in designing the band's pregame and halftime shows, and he arranged the music the band played on the field. He was known to have a talent for "writing to the band's strengths." Before coming to LSU, Tyra gained teaching experience as band director at Lincoln Senior High School, Des Moines, Iowa, for one year and as band director at Morton Junior College, Cicero, Illinois, for one semester. He accepted an invitation to serve as staff arranger for the U.S. Navy School of Music, Washington, DC, for the 1956–1957 school term. The experience he gained there refined his arranging skills, developing them to a professional level.

Tyra's tenure as director of the Tiger Band began just three weeks before the start of school and the 1958 football season. He could not have imagined the organizational challenges he and his "post-fire" student band staff would face. They had inherited the task of putting together a complicated puzzle with some missing pieces. Prior to registration, the size and instrumentation of the Tiger Band could only be roughly estimated, and charting formations and music arrangements for halftime of the home opening game could not be solidified. Final registration figures revealed that ninety-three students had enrolled in the 1958 Tiger Band. Until construction of the new band complex was complete, the band's temporary indoor home was a large room adjacent to the ROTC rifle-firing range in the basement of the Gym Armory. On the bright side, most of the new band instruments ordered after the Band House fire arrived promptly, and the replacement uniforms were promised for delivery before LSU's home opener on October 4.

In normal times, charting formations and arranging music for the band's halftime performances of the coming year usually began soon after the conclusion of football season and continued through the spring and summer terms. However, in 1958, times were anything but normal for Tyra and the Tiger Band. In an era before computers were available to facilitate the charting of formations, the process was tedious and time-consuming, requiring many hours to complete. Considering the circumstances, it is remarkable that Tyra was able to sustain his efforts for the duration of the football season.

The 1958 season ended memorably, with LSU ranked number one in the United Press International football poll. As national football champions, the Tigers accepted an invitation to play Clemson in the Sugar Bowl Classic in New Orleans on New Year's Day, 1959. After performing at five home games and two away games, the Tiger Band successfully ended its first season under Tyra's direction with a halftime appearance in the Sugar Bowl, televised nationally by NBC. Reminiscing several months later, Tyra graciously credited members of his student staff for the help and support, above and beyond the call of duty, they gave him in "surviving" his first football season at LSU.[3]

THE ADVENT OF GOLDEN TRADITIONS

Tyra was promoted to director of the LSU Band on July 1, 1959, when Jones stepped down to teach full-time. At age twenty-six, Tyra was the youngest director of a major university band in America. A new, exciting era in the band's story began with his appointment, and his brief tenure would be one of the most productive periods since the band's founding. Tyra's innovational creativity shaped the band's development well into the next century. Having successfully completed his first year at LSU, with his feet now firmly planted on the ground and with his recent promotion, Tyra gave his creative impulses free rein. For example, since his earliest days at LSU, he felt that the marching band should have a title in addition to its time-honored name. Drawing upon the school colors and the gold trim of the bandsmen's uniforms for inspiration, he instinctively divined the perfect title: "The Golden Band from Tigerland."

THE GOLDEN GIRLS

Before the 1958 football season ended, Tyra conceptualized the creation of a new, expanded dance line trained by a professional choreographer. His idea crystallized by the following spring, and planning for this novel addition to the band began in earnest. One of the first dancers selected, Glenda Garr Lofton, recalled in 1990 that she was there when Tyra conceived the Golden Girls. "Purdue has its Golden Girl, he said, and LSU will have its Golden Girls. He called us the Ballet Corps, however, and I shall never forget," said Lofton, "when our picture appeared on the front page of the *Sunday Advocate* with the headline 'Ballerinas to Make Debut on the Football Field.'" Word of the dance line quickly spread on campus and around Baton Rouge. A *Baton Rouge State Times* article introducing the Ballet Corps sensationalized the dance line and raised interest

left: The first *Gumbo* photograph of the Ballet Corps. (*Gumbo* 1960)

right: The drum major confers with the Tigerettes. (*Gumbo* 1959)

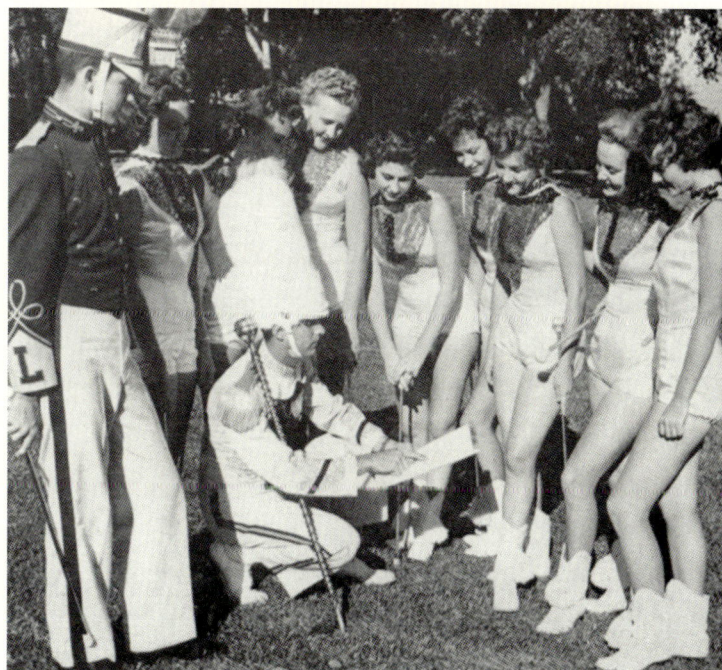

Tyra's 1961 routines for the Ballet Corps incorporated props. (OPRR)

in LSU's latest edition of football showmanship even higher. "Louisiana State University has a new offering this fall—a ballet corps. Ballet Corps! You read it right the first time! LSU's director of bands, Tom Tyra, is completely undaunted by the possibility that football mixes with ballet, like alcohol with gasoline."[4]

Mary Elizabeth Norckauer, a former performer and choreographer with Holiday on Ice, became the first choreographer to direct the Ballet Corps. Hired as an assistant professor in the university's physical education department, which included dance, she agreed to work with Tyra and the newly formed Ballet Corps, realizing that she was taking on two full-time jobs. In 2009 she recalled the group's first appearance at a football game. Before presenting their Broadway-style dance routines, the young women stood on the press box sideline at halftime wearing purple capes over outfits of gold lamé and sequins with easily detachable skirts. For their entry onto the field, the band played a special fanfare written by Tyra. "At that moment and in sync with the fanfare, the girls opened their capes and one by one, dropped them to the ground. The place went crazy! We were told that binocular sales skyrocketed in Baton Rouge that year, and the stadium concession stand sales started going down at halftime because everyone was staying in the stands to watch the Ballet Corps."[5]

In 1965, the name of the Ballet Corps was changed to the Golden Girls. It is estimated that on their fiftieth anniversary in 2009, more than eight hundred female LSU students had danced with the line. Since their founding, the Golden Girls have entertained and thrilled LSU students and Tiger football fans across America with their talent and style.

PREGAME

Today, LSU football fans take the band's pregame performances for granted—after all, they have been part of Tiger football lore for over half a century—but there were few pregame ceremonies at LSU games before Tyra became director of bands. He had attended Northwestern University, where it was customary for marching bands in the Big Ten Conference schools to "take the field" before games. Upon coming to LSU, Tyra was surprised to discover that the Tiger Band always played the National Anthem from its seats in the stadium. Like other bands of the Southeastern Conference schools, it seldom ventured onto the field for pregame ceremonies. Tyra felt that pregame pageantry at LSU was long overdue, and he established this new tradition beginning with the game against Rice on September 19, 1959. Under the bright lights of Tiger Stadium, forty-eight thousand spectators witnessed the birth of one of the Tiger Band's most cherished traditions: "Pregame, LSU."

THE TIGER MASCOT

Off and on over the years, photographs of students dressed in homemade tiger suits had appeared in LSU's yearbook, the *Gumbo*. Most often they depict the tiger leading a live goat, representing Tulane University's mascot, onto the football field. But there had never been a band-sanctioned costumed student mascot for LSU. The idea of an LSU bandsman masquerading as a tiger was another brainchild of Tyra's. During the 1958 Sugar Bowl, the Clemson band's tiger mascot attracted Tyra's attention and generated an impressive response from the spectators. While attending an LSU basketball game in Parker Coliseum about a month after the Clemson game, Tyra was surprised to find one of his own bandsmen, Silvain Tauzy, cavorting around the ball court wearing a

The drum major strikes a pose in front of Memorial Tower, 1960. (LSU Band)

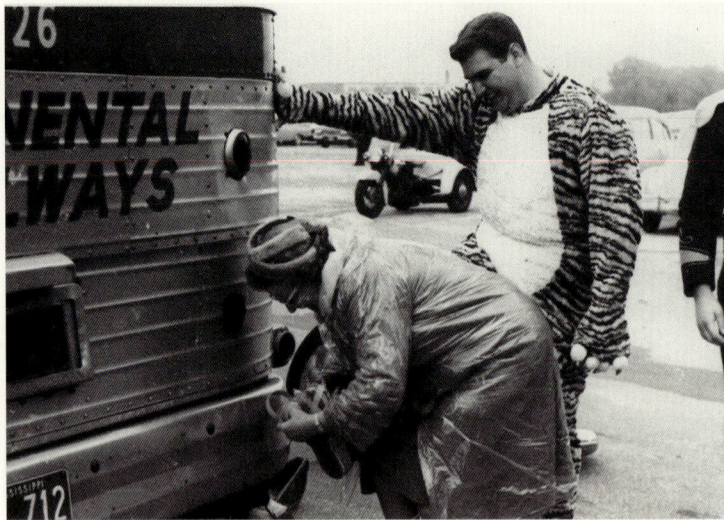

Mrs. Tauzy helps her son with his mascot suit. (Photograph by Johnny Gordon)

homemade tiger costume. Tyra later learned that Tauzy's mother had created the outfit for her son to wear while taking part in one of the basketball pep band's skits. Witnessing Tauzy's impact on the basketball fans and realizing that it was similar to that of Clemson's mascot on the Sugar Bowl crowd, Tyra immediately grasped the potential entertainment value of the antics of a college student clad as a make-believe tiger. Tyra asked Tauzy to become the Tiger Band's mascot. The young man readily agreed, and by the beginning of football season, a professionally designed costume had been produced for him. It was delivered to the Band Department, C.O.D., on September 18, 1959, the day before the home opener with Rice.

On the evening of the game, Mike III, LSU's real tiger, made his traditional ride around the stadium field to the cheers and applause of students and the Tiger faithful. After rousing the crowd and attempting to intimidate the Rice football players, he was returned, as usual, to his permanent home across from Tiger Stadium. Minutes before halftime, Tauzy, in full mascot regalia, climbed into Mike's mobile cage and was whisked into Tiger Stadium. No announcement had been made to the spectators that they were soon to be introduced to a second LSU mascot. At midpoint of the band's halftime performance, the cage, with what appeared to be Mike III snugly ensconced within, was moved to the juncture of the fifty-yard marker and the west sideline. On cue and with great fanfare, Tauzy popped out of the cage, creating not only a sensation but also a moment of horror for the fans seated in the west side's lowest rows. Many of them were completely fooled by the costumed mascot and thought that LSU's real tiger had been unintentionally released. In a blink, fright gave way to relief and then to a shower of cheers as the spectators roared with delight and approval. Thanks to Tyra and Tauzy, for the first time in school history, LSU had not one, but two live mascots.[6]

A NEW BAND HALL

Architectural planning for the band's new complex began within weeks of the disastrous Band House fire. The band's new home consisted of a wing joined to the west end of the Music and Dramatic Arts building and a large rehearsal hall connected to the wing by a covered walk. The new band complex opened in September 1959. The wing was built of rock that harmonized with other buildings on campus and contained rooms for ensemble and sectional rehearsals. The large rehearsal hall contained a rehearsal room for the band, administrative offices, music library, instrument repair shop, and storage rooms. Offices and the music library were located on the second floor, opening onto a balcony that projected out and over the rehearsal hall. The new band complex far surpassed its predecessors in every way. At the time, it was one of the few buildings on campus with central air and heat. Importantly, the building's rehearsal hall was well designed acoustically and could comfortably accommodate a band of 225 members.[7] The 1959 Tiger Band had a membership of 128, with growth projected to 200 by the

The Tiger Band Hall, constructed in 1959 adjacent to the Music and Dramatic Arts building. (OPRR)

1964 football season. Neither the university administrators nor the school's architects could see into the future and envision the truly gigantic bands that would emerge in the next two decades. By the late 1980s, the band complex would prove to be spatially inadequate for the band's needs.

THE MUSIC

As Tyra began planning the Tiger Band's first pregame performance in the fall of 1959, he selected "Touchdown for LSU" as the band's entrance and downfield marching music and set about creating a new arrangement of the piece. Staff informed him that Carazo and the late Senator Long had composed "Touchdown" and that Carazo had made the original arrangement himself. To avoid offending Carazo, who had resided in Baton Rouge since his days at LSU, Tyra visited with him and asked his permission to produce a new arrangement of "Touchdown" to be tailored closely to the instrumentation of the 1959 Tiger Band. Carazo graciously granted Tyra's request, and strains of the new version of "Touchdown for LSU" echoed through Tiger Stadium as the Tiger Band took the field in its first pregame show.

An unusual set of circumstances surrounded the acquisition of LSU's best-known and most popular school song, "Hey, Fightin' Tigers." The university's athletic director, Jim Corbett, and his wife visited New York in 1962 and attended several of Broadway's hit musicals, including *Wildcat.* Corbett was mesmerized by its show-stopping tune "Hey, Look Me Over." At some point he realized that the song would be a terrific addition to LSU's repertory of school songs. Corbett contacted the producer of *Wildcat* and requested that LSU be granted exclusive rights to incorporate the melody of "Hey, Look Me Over" into a school song. Eventually, permission was granted, and according to the agreement, no other university or college would ever be permitted to adopt the melody for its own purposes. Corbett had delivered a grand new song to LSU's football tradition—singlehandedly, but for Gene Quaw. Quaw, who had served as the university's composer and producer of campus musicals since 1939, had retired and was living in Montana at the time. Nevertheless, Corbett persuaded him to render one further service. Quaw's lyrics transformed "Hey, Look Me Over" into the unforgettable "Hey, Fightin' Tigers."[8] It has surpassed "Touchdown for LSU" and "Fight for LSU" in popularity, and many students and alumni mistakenly believe that it is the university's official fight song. When it is played at football games, the voices of thousands of students singing Quaw's lyrics all but drown out the band's powerful sound. With some modification, the arrangement of "Hey, Fightin' Tigers" that Tyra created in 1962 is still used today.

During his tenure as the Tiger Band's director, Tyra devoted much of his time and energy to arranging music for the band's pregame and halftime performances. Although arranging for a major university marching band is a full-time job in itself, Tyra viewed it as simply one more necessary task. In all, he created more than two hundred arrangements for the Tiger Band's forty-two home games and bowl appearances in the years from 1959 through 1963. In a 1959 interview, Tyra shared insights into what the work of a band director entailed. He and the assistant directors spent more than seven hundred hours on each football show—planning and charting band formations, writing original music, clearing copyrights, and ordering props, among other tasks. There was also the hazard of viewing formations from a forty-foot tower mounted on wheels that on a windy day could move five yards down the field with him on it.[9]

TYRA RESIGNS

Over six years, Tyra actively recruited students for the band and succeeded in enlisting them in large numbers. By the 1963 football season, Tyra's final year as director, the Tiger Band's membership had nearly doubled in size; at 170, it was the largest marching band in the Southeastern Conference. In a letter dated April 3, 1964, to the dean of the School of Music, Everett Timm, Tyra unexpectedly resigned his position as band director. Because of the many unresolved problems resulting from the devastating Band House fire and the timing of his appointment as director just weeks before the start of the 1958 football season, Tyra had experienced the most difficult first year on the job of any director in the band's history. At the age of twenty-five and with virtually no teaching or conducting experience, but with the uncanny exuberance of youth, he confronted and successfully met the challenges of his new position. Tyra completed the work, begun by Jones, of rebuilding LSU's postwar marching band and returning it to national prominence. It could be fairly argued that except for the equally brief tenure of Carazo, never before or since in the story of the Tiger Band had so much been accomplished by one person in so short a time.

Night aerial of "LSU" spelled on field by the band. (LSU Band)

Band formation featuring the Colorguard. (LSU Band)

California or bust: The Tiger Band was determined to win. (OPRR)

5

THE ALL-AMERICAN COLLEGE TV BAND

1964–1977

The debilitating years of World War II and the disastrous Band House fire of 1958 had left two men with the daunting tasks of reorganizing and rebuilding a devastated, demoralized band. L. Bruce Jones, the first of the two, older and more experienced, had reestablished the organization's national reputation. The second, Tom Tyra, younger and more creative, restored its physical base and energized the spirits of its members. Their accomplishments set the stage for the next of LSU's band directors, different in many respects from any who had come before. He was a man of unusual intellect and talent, as comfortable exploring the mysteries of mathematics and architecture as in solving the exigencies of a marching band's gridiron performance. As William F. Swor's students and colleagues quickly learned, he was an entirely different breed of band director. In a few short years, he guided the Golden Band from Tigerland to the heights of national renown and into its second golden age.

WILLIAM F. SWOR

Prior to coming to LSU, William F. "Bill" Swor (1927–2004), a Shreveport native, led the award-winning Alfred I. duPont High School Band of Jacksonville, Florida, from 1954 to 1964. Swor's son said his father attended a seminary in Shreveport, where he developed a passion for music. Swor received bachelor of science and master of arts degrees from Peabody Teachers' College and a doctorate in musical arts from the University of Texas at Austin. For two years he taught at Peabody, then directed a high school band in a Tennessee school and played the clarinet in the Nashville Symphony. After leaving LSU, Swor taught music and directed the band of North Clayton High School in College Park, Georgia, a suburb of Atlanta. He spent the last twenty years of his life in Atlanta.[1]

Excerpts from Tiger Band handbooks and travel itineraries created by Swor during his twelve years as director of the Tiger Band give a glimpse of his complex personality. His obsession with control and pedantic attention to the smallest detail, so evident in page after page of memos to the bandsmen, are character traits that marked every facet of his professional life. Some of those who worked closely with him stated that these were the chief factors that contributed to his remarkable success in guiding the Golden Band from Tigerland to the first of its two national honors.

Each fall Swor sent written directives to members of the auxiliary groups and the band. His golden rule was, "Don't Be on Time—Be Early!!!" He focused on care of the uniforms; halftime perfection, especially for bowl games; personal responsibilities while traveling to away games; and performance expectations. Swor had strict rules about personal appearance. When the bandsmen were traveling, he instructed them to "take pride in their appearance, to be clean and sharp looking. The men should have a close haircut, no long sideburns and well-trimmed mustaches. No one should appear in hotel lobbies in improper attire." The women should never be seen with rollers in their hair or wearing bermuda shorts. Swor wanted to dismiss bandsman Del Moon because of the length of his hair, but Moon proposed a compromise that Swor accepted. Whenever Moon appeared with the band, he tucked his long hair under a short wig.

Swor's strongest demands regarded the quality of performance and how the bandsmen should achieve perfection. He was particularly concerned about halftime routines that were broadcast to millions of people on national television. "You certainly do not want all of their attention drawn to you because you goof. With the proper self-discipline at halftime, you must place yourselves in the proper frame of mind to do a beautiful job." Swor encouraged the band members to concentrate on sound and the correlation of their footwork with the music. It was important for the bandsmen to have constant awareness of "good alignment, delayed pivots, appropriate step style, high-peak halts, instrument moves and other pivot technics." Perfect alignment was a

Bill Swor became band director in 1964. (LSU Band)

left: **Precision performance, 1973.** (LSU Band)

right: **Accurate steps, 1974.** (LSU Band)

detail that would add artistry to their presentation of the LSU "sound." "Let's make the Tiger Band the outstanding band across the nation. This must be our finest performance ever!"[2]

Years after his tenure at LSU had ended, Swor surprised everyone by displaying a sense of humor and a true admiration for the Tiger Alumni Band when he spoke at their second reunion banquet in 1987. Swor told the alumni that they had achieved perfection during their years: "For those of you who were here during the 'Swor' era (not error), you may recall the hazards of our drill system. I trust that you will always remember my kind and gentle manner, how understanding I always was, and how sympathetic I was to your problems and excuses. That I was never unreasonably demanding and how very tolerant I always was with any faux pas you might have bestowed upon our performance. You're not buying this, are you?" Swor was not unaware of his obsession with perfection, which he had imposed on the bandsmen.[3]

BAND NIGHT AND THE INVITATIONAL MARCHING BAND FESTIVAL

In his first three years at LSU, Swor carried on the popular tradition of Band Night. On Saturday, October 10, 1964, he and the Tiger Band hosted three thousand young musicians from fifty-eight high school bands. At halftime of the LSU–North Carolina football game, the massed bands literally covered the length and breadth of the football field as they formed the familiar "LSU." The high school bandsmen and the Tiger Band serenaded sixty-three thousand spectators with LSU's school songs and the patriotic air "God of Our Fathers," all conducted by Swor.

The seventeen-year custom of LSU's Annual Band Night came to an end on October 1, 1966. The final massed band performance was held in Tiger Stadium during halftime of the LSU-Miami football game. The Invitational Marching Band Festival would supplant it.

The first Invitational Marching Band Festival was held on the field of LSU's Bernie Moore Track Stadium on October 14, 1967. Swor invited ten of Louisiana's outstanding high school marching bands in classifications A, AA, and AAA to compete in the festival. The Lafayette High School Band won top honors in the competition. That night, the victorious band repeated its performance at halftime of the LSU-Miami football game.

In July 1968, Swor announced to Louisiana's high school band directors that Band Night had been discontinued in favor of the recently instituted marching festival. "Last fall we conducted the first LSU Invitational Marching Band Festival which, by virtue of its success, will now become an annual affair," he wrote. "The goal of this festival is to improve the standards of the State's high school marching bands." In 1970 the competition was expanded to include twenty of Louisiana's best high school marching bands, and its name was changed to the LSU Marching Band Festival. Thousands of spectators flocked to LSU's track stadium to watch the state's finest marching bands perform and compete. Year by year, the event's popularity grew. In the ninth and final contest on December 6, 1975, the Acadiana High School Band of Lafayette placed first and repeated its winning routine in Tiger Stadium at halftime of the Grantland Rice Bowl game.[4]

above: **Practicing for Band Night at the Bernie Moore Track Stadium. (Photograph by Ray Maurer, ca. 1972; OPRR)**

facing page: **Massed high school bands spell "LSU" across the field for the annual Band Night. (LSU Band)**

BAND AUXILIARIES

Although Tyra modeled the Ballet Corps on Purdue's Golden Girl in 1959, it received its name, Golden Girls, from Swor. One of Swor's first acts in 1964 was to formalize the name change. Swor also made the twirling corps' name, the Tigerettes, official.

In 1965, new uniforms arrived for the band and its auxiliaries for the season football opener. Also in that year, Swor created a squad of fifteen coeds who carried banners representing LSU's fifteen degree-granting schools and colleges. As his concept for the banner-carrying group evolved, he renamed it the Guidon Corps in 1966 and in 1971 revised its organization. At the LSU-Florida football game on October 9, 1971, twelve coeds dressed in white skirts and jackets trimmed with purple and gold made their debut as members of the "Flag Corps."

The Ballet Corps was renamed the Golden Girls in 1964. (JFP)

The members of the reorganized Flag Corps were chosen from the band's existing membership because they had marching experience. Ten of them carried the flags of the Southeastern Conference's ten schools, with two more women bearing white flags. Carol Weathersby Larsen served as captain and developed the routines. Larsen recalled in 2011 that the tall metal flagpoles with spiked tips that Swor chose for the women to carry were so heavy that they wore white leather straps with a cup to support their poles. They did not attempt to twirl the flags. In typical Swor fashion, the director prohibited the flags from touching the ground.[5] Since 1971, the name of the unit has changed from "Flag Corps" to "Flag Line" and finally to "Colorguard."

top left: Golden Girls, 2009, wearing a replica of the 1964 costumes. (Photograph by Rachel Saltzberg)

top right: Scarlet Searle (*left*), a Tigerette, and Karen Cavanaugh (*right*), a Golden Girl, with Randy Babin modeling the new band uniform for 1965. (OPRR)

left: The Tiger Band's Flag Line, 1965. (OPRR)

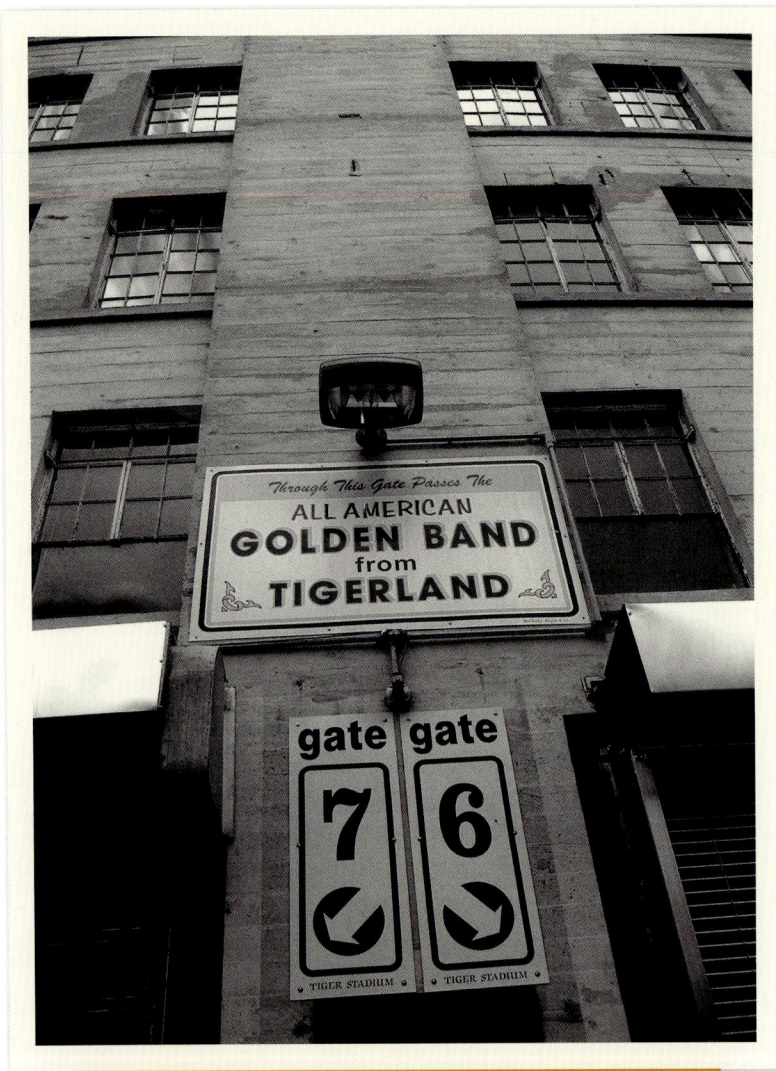

Stadium sign: "Through This Gate Passes the All American Golden Band from Tigerland." (LSU Band)

PREGAME CHANGES

What exactly makes the Tiger Band's pregame performance so memorable? Who can explain the magic? Pregame in Tiger Stadium must be seen and heard and felt first-hand, for in no other way can its enigmatic power to arouse and excite be truly comprehended. In his first season as director, Swor knew he wanted to change the original pregame format designed by Tyra and to "tailor a one-of-a-kind program specifically for LSU . . . something new, something that would startle everyone." No other SEC university bands in 1964 had developed a standardized, custom-designed opening routine such as Swor conceptualized and created. His something new and startling quickly took root and has remained basically intact since 1964, with only superficial alterations. Over the years, the Tiger Band's pregame performances are as anticipated, as popular, and as beloved as ever.

THE ALL-AMERICAN COLLEGE TV BAND

During the 1970 football season, the Chevrolet Motor Division of General Motors Corporation, a longtime supporter of NCAA football, sponsored a national television band contest to identify the most outstanding university marching band in America. Competing bands were evaluated in four general categories—playing, uniformity, marching, and general effect—for a maximum of one hundred points. In addition to a panel of six university adjudicators, seven celebrities in the world of music and entertainment also served as judges: Doc Severinsen, Pete Fountain, Steve Allen, Herb Alpert, Les Brown, Duke Ellington, and Meredith Willson. The procedure for evaluating the competing bands involved "live" on-site judging by three adjudicators and "film" judging of regional or national telecast games not on the "live" adjudicating schedule. The winner of the contest was to be named by Chevrolet as the "All-American College TV Band." First prize was an all-expense-paid trip to the East-West Shrine Game on January 2, 1971, in Oakland, California. The selected winner, the LSU Tiger Band, was featured in an uninterrupted halftime performance and presentation of a trophy during the television broadcast of the game.

The Tiger Band also marched in the Orange Bowl parade the night of December 31, 1970. Chevrolet's advertising manager felt the back-to-back appearances of the LSU Band in Miami on Friday and in San Francisco/Oakland on Saturday would "add an extra dimension of interest" to their program. The Tiger Band's cross-country flight was the first ever made by an American university band.[6]

OTHER HIGHLIGHTS OF THE SWOR YEARS

Swor sought performance opportunities to increase the band's public relations value. During his first season, on October 9, 1964, the Tiger Band greeted President Lyndon Baines Johnson at the New Orleans International Airport and serenaded the president

with "Hail to the Chief" as he disembarked Air Force One. The band was invited to play on September 18, 1966, before the Houston Oilers game against the Giants in the Houston Astrodome. The *Bonham Daily Favorite* headline for the game announcement told fans not to miss the LSU Band or the game. The *Houston Post* declared the event the best band performance ever held in the Astrodome. Again in September 1968, the Tiger Band performed in the Astrodome.[7]

The LSU football team won the inaugural Peach Bowl in Atlanta in December 1968, but the press gave highest honors to the Tiger Band. The band led the pregame parade and put on a great halftime show in cold rain and mud, prompting the *Atlanta News Report* to say it had "won" the halftime show. In 1972 Swor staged a halftime tribute to former band director Castro Carazo. From 1964 through 1975, during the years when college football halftime shows received full coverage during televised games, the Tiger Band was featured on twenty-five national broadcasts.

left: Johnny Gordon, holding drumsticks, concentrates on the game in 1965. (Photograph courtesy of Johnny Gordon)

right: Bandsmen relax after all their hard work, 1965. (Photograph by Johnny Gordon)

CONFLICTS

In 1970 Athletic Director Carl Maddox said that the Tiger Band boosted the morale of the football players, who recognized the band as their staunchest, most loyal source of support. Maddox's backing of the Tiger Band lessened, however, as Swor's demands on the Athletic Department budget grew year by year. Maddox also found Swor less

Cheering the team while wearing new uniforms, 1973. (BDFP)

than cooperative, even while he tried to find ways to increase the band's funding. In 1973 LSU chancellor Cecil Taylor asked the Athletic Department to pay for new band uniforms and promised to refund a quarter of the cost from university general funds at year's end. Athletics also subsidized the band's travel to away games and the 1973 Miami Orange Bowl game. But Swor argued that more money was needed for travel expenses. If the sole purpose of the marching band was to perform at fall football games, said Maddox, then the band should be operated by Athletics with the band and its director under his oversight. Otherwise, he argued, the School of Music should appropriate funds necessary for band operations and not rely so heavily upon Athletics.[8]

Swor regularly admonished the bandsmen to seek perfection, to maintain a cooperative attitude, and to exercise discipline. He had difficulty applying his rules to his own conduct, even though he was fighting for the benefit of the Tiger Band. He wanted any qualified student to receive a place in the band, because, as he put it, the band represented the entire university. Swor pressed for additional funding, instruments, and uniforms but was continually denied. A downturn in the state economy in the 1970s caused financial difficulties for Louisiana universities, and administrators worked to contain costs in all areas—including the Tiger Band. Miscommunication among Swor, the administration, and Athletics, to the detriment of the Tiger Band, raged on. While on sabbatical for the academic year 1976–77, Swor nevertheless wrote to administrators about band service awards remaining static even as student fees rose. Before the end of his sabbatical, the ranks had closed against him. He was dismissed as director of bands in June 1977.[9]

It cannot be denied that Swor raised the Tiger Band to new heights of achievement. His positive influence brought about the band's second golden age. Under his direction, it won the All-American College TV Band Award. Swor improved the band's style and performance, brought African American students into the organization, and fought, even at a significant personal cost, for needed improvements and financial support.

Dr. John Sibley Butler, Outstanding LSU Alumnus of the Year for 2012 and a former bandsman, praised Swor:

Many former directors of LSU's marching bands have been distinguished in their own special ways; however, in my opinion, among all who came before him, William F. "Bill" Swor stands alone. In his twelve years, he redefined the stature of the Tiger Band on the national stage. Its deserved reputation as America's finest collegiate marching band evolved from Bill Swor's unique ability to conceptualize, coordinate and integrate extremely complex precision drills with phenomenal arrangements of the very best in classical music. My first introduction to Mr. Swor came in 1965 at the beginning of my freshman year at LSU. To this day I'm not quite sure whether I was admitted to membership in Tiger Band because my audition met with his approval, or simply because the band was in dire need of trombone players. I suspect it was the latter. During the following four years I learned quite a lot about precision marching, and I like to think that I even developed into a pretty good trombone player. However, there were other lessons Mr. Swor taught me which proved to be of much greater importance and value, and, which would serve me well for a lifetime. Now, I can sum up the themes of these in three simple concepts—preparation, confidence and execution. The many lessons embedded in each of these have formed the foundation upon which my life, personal and professional, has been built.

Over the course of many years, the lessons he taught me in Tiger Band have remained with me. They have influenced the development of my character and impacted my life profoundly.[10]

John Sibley Butler. (Photograph courtesy of John Sibley Butler)

The 1993 Tiger Band forms the team's entrance tunnel. (LSU Band)

The 2007 Parade of Champions, celebrating a winning year for the LSU Tigers and the Southern Jaguars. (LSU Band)

A star formation typical of Rouse/Swor halftime performances. (BDFP)

6

THE BAND IN TRANSITION

1978–1980

Since its founding in 1893, the LSU Band has had numerous dedicated, talented directors. In the modern era, two of the most successful of these were Bill Swor and Frank Wickes. The bridge between these giants of the band world was the four-year directorship of Nicholas M. Rouse. Although illness cut short Rouse's tenure, one truly remarkable accomplishment distinguished it. During the football seasons of 1978 and 1979, he led the Tiger Band through a complex, difficult process of transition that transformed its marching style.

Rouse, standing, assists Swor with field formation charts. (OPRR)

NICHOLAS M. ROUSE

Nicholas M. (Nick) Rouse (1936–1993), a native of New Orleans, moved to Baton Rouge in 1954, where he enrolled at Istrouma High School and played alto saxophone in the band. He entered LSU majoring in music education and in his second year was selected as the Tiger Band's drum major, serving in the position for three years. Rouse took a job as director of the Redemptorist High School Band while an undergraduate and continued as its director until his graduation in 1963. From 1964 to 1967, he directed bands at Robert E. Lee High School and Istrouma High School in Baton Rouge before returning to LSU to pursue a master's degree in music education. Swor chose Rouse as his graduate assistant, a position that required him to chart all the formations that the band presented in gridiron performances. Encouraged by Coach Press Maravich, Rouse also led the basketball pep band. Made up of twenty-six volunteers from the Tiger Band, this group was named the Court Jesters. Attired in striped coats and straw hats, the pep band performed at the games along with a group called the "Pom Pom Girls," who danced and led cheers.[1]

After graduate school, Rouse was appointed director of the Denham Springs High School Band in 1968. When Swor took a leave of absence from LSU in 1976, he recommended Rouse as his replacement on a one-year appointment as acting director of bands.

Rouse struggled with limited staff resources. In comparison to the staffs of other major university bands of the mid- to late 1970s, LSU's band staff could be described as bare-boned. It consisted of a music arranger, an instrument repair technician, three graduate assistants, and a secretary. The graduate assistants were responsible for the field design and charting of the Tiger Band's halftime performances. Despite the difficulties of managing the bands, at the end of 1976 Chancellor Paul Murrill expressed his thanks to Rouse for his effectiveness as acting band director. Murrill said he and others at the university appreciated "the professional and efficient way in which you assumed these responsibilities."[2]

When Swor was dismissed the following year, Rouse was named director of bands and placed in charge of LSU's varied band programs, including the 260-member Tiger Marching Band.[3] In the capacity of director of bands, Rouse conducted the Tiger Band, the Symphonic Band, the Concert Band, the Wind Ensemble, the Jazz Ensemble, the Summer Starlight Band, and the Basketball Band. In addition, he taught a graduate course in conducting and an undergraduate class in marching band techniques. Rouse also began the push for improvements to the Band Hall.

AN EVOLVING HALFTIME FORMAT

Over time, the Tiger Band's halftime performances had gradually evolved into a somewhat monotonous blend of block-band marching and pageantry. By 1964, Swor had abandoned the timeworn block-band drill and replaced it with avant-garde, extremely

The Court Jesters, led by Rouse (*seated front row, wearing dark jacket*), in 1965. (OPRR)

complex company-front precision marching, unmatched in its levels of difficulty and perfection. By the mid-1970s, however, Swor's innovation had also run its course.

As the novelty of company-front precision drill began to wane, a very different kind of gridiron entertainment emerged in university bands across the country. With roots planted decades in the past, "corps style" marching arrived with a flourish. Rouse, sensing change in the air, determined that LSU's Tiger Band would not be left behind. He understood that the transition to an unfamiliar style would be difficult and possibly even disastrous. Much to his credit and with the help of his small staff, Rouse accepted the challenge the transition presented.

The implementation of the "glide step" radically changed the look of the Tiger Band. Different from the high leg lift of the "peak" step, it was a smooth, low-to-the-ground stride with the heel rather than the toe touching the ground first. By absorbing much of

left: Uniformity was always a goal for the marching band, ca. 1979. (LSU Band)

right: Practice, practice, practice for the drum line. (LSU Band)

facing page: Under Rouse, the Golden Girls, as well as the Tigerettes and Flag Corps, were incorporated into the pregame and halftime band programs. (LSU Band)

the shock caused by contact of toe and turf, the glide step allowed bandsmen to maintain a near-motionless upper body while marching. This cushioning effect minimized the constant jarring of the brass instruments' mouthpieces against tender lips and thus increased the musicians' staying power. With time and practice, the bandsmen soon began to execute the glide step with precision. As they did so, an unexpected visual effect occurred. Moving from point to point on the gridiron, the musicians appeared to spectators to be floating rather than marching.[4]

In corps-style presentation, playing and marching are equal partners. The musical and visual effects of the performance are integrated so harmoniously that one is never allowed to overshadow the other. John Edmunds, the band's arranger, scored the halftime music to achieve maximum musical effect from the first to last notes of each show. Mike Strasser, graduate assistant responsible for field design and charting, devised drill sequences that took full advantage of Edmunds's powerful arrangements. The two men worked closely together to tailor the music to the complex patterns constantly emerging on the field.

In the corps style, the percussion section, referred to in the vernacular as the "drum line," is the heart and soul of the modern marching band presentation. As Rouse envisioned the Tiger Band, the drum line differed from the more traditional percussion section both in sheer size and in novelty of instrumentation. It incorporated more players and a wider variety of instruments, including such gridiron exotics as xylophones, stationed on the sidelines. During performance, members of the drum line were grouped together, usually at the center of the band on the field. This strategic placement of the

percussionists improved the rhythmic unity of several hundred bandsmen spread over the breadth of the football field. From the start of the Tiger Band's transition process, the drum line emerged as a featured auxiliary in halftime performances.

THE ROLE OF AUXILIARIES

The Tiger Band's move to a corps-style format transformed the traditional roles of its three auxiliary units. Previously the Golden Girls, the Tigerettes, and the Flag Corps had been treated more or less as mere add-ons to the band's halftime entertainment. Rouse saw them as integral parts of the whole and elevated them to a new role as equal partners with the band, featuring them throughout the halftime performances. For the first time in its history, the Tiger Band and its auxiliaries were one!

Rouse improved the auxiliaries in other ways as well, most notably by attempting to broaden their diversity. By 1965 African American students were members of the Tiger Band and sports teams, but as late as 1979 no African American students participated in the band's auxiliaries. In October 1976, Chancellor Murrill asked Rouse to audition black students for those groups, and six months later Rouse reported that he had initiated procedures with the assistance of LSU's affirmative action officer. The black students who were already members of the band had also assisted, and five women were recruited to audition for the Golden Girls. Rouse gained the support of a black instructor in women's health and physical education to serve with him as a judge for the tryouts. Videotaped auditions, rather than live tryouts, were held, which Rouse hoped would "satisfy the University responsibility regarding Title VI."[5]

In June 1979, Rouse reported to Murrill on "his not-yet-rewarding efforts with the enlistment of black girls" in the Golden Girls, the Flag Corps, and the Tigerettes, even though he had advice on possible solutions from the Student Government Association's Black Affairs chairman and Black Greeks representative, and the director of LSU's Equal Opportunity Programs.[6] A new director, Rouse's successor, would eventually bring diversity to the membership of the band's auxiliaries.

ROUSE RESIGNS

In the years of his tenure, Rouse transformed the marching style of the Tiger Band. With help from a small staff, he presided over the band's successful transition to the "new look" that has endured for nearly four decades. The halftime spectacles presented by the Golden Band from Tigerland, a refined reflection of Rouse's vision and creation, never fail to thrill and excite LSU football fans. For health reasons, Nick Rouse's brief time as the university's director of bands came to a premature conclusion with his resignation on June 30, 1980.[7]

Champions, 2004, for the 2003 season. *Sports Illustrated* shows the band on the field.
(Photographer Jamie Squire/ SPO 2844098 LSU v Oklahoma/Getty Images)

Pregame 2005 before game with Florida. (LSU Band)

The view for the band in formation. (LSU Band)

The Colorguard, front and center of the Tiger Band.
(Photograph by Rachel Saltzberg)

7

THE WICKES YEARS

1980–2010

Prior to 1980, the LSU Tiger Band had experienced two distinct periods of recognition and fame on the national stage. From a strictly historical perspective, both epochs have frequently been referred to as the band's golden ages. Alfred Wickboldt, a well-grounded musician and stern disciplinarian, and Castro Carazo, a gifted composer and flamboyant showman, ushered in the first. Each enjoyed the encouragement, support, and collaboration of Louisiana's enigmatic populist governor and U.S. senator, Huey Pierce Long. In these men's short-lived heyday, the LSU Band traveled widely and received acclaim everywhere it appeared. A world war began and ended and three decades passed before another director, one obsessed with attention to detail and driven to achieve perfection, would guide the band once again to the pinnacle of national renown and into its second golden age. In 1970, under the direction of William F. Swor, the Golden Band from

Tigerland was named the country's best university marching band as its unmatched gridiron performance earned it the title of All-American College TV Band.

One decade later, Frank B. Wickes was appointed LSU's director of bands. His thirty-year tenure was remarkable for its unprecedented length and was defined by the quality of its accomplishments. Those who worked closely with Wickes learned that he was an extremely gifted musician and a conductor and teacher of the highest caliber. They also discovered that he had exceptional organizational skills and an unflagging work ethic. These personal traits characterized the man who, year by year, methodically crafted a university band department equal in excellence to any in America. Wickes's predecessors transformed LSU's band in their own time and in their own ways. Following in their footsteps and with the help of a team of talented, dedicated, colleagues, Wickes presided over the Tiger Band's third golden age.

FRANK B. WICKES

Frank B. Wickes, oldest son of Rupert and Frances Wickes, was born in Ticonderoga, New York, on August 8, 1937. Frances Johnston Wickes, a musical prodigy, studied piano at the prestigious New England Conservatory of Music. She was recognized as a classical artist on piano and organ, and as a magnificent jazz pianist with an innate ability to improvise. Wickes believes that he inherited his love of, and talent for, music from his mother. The family moved to Ocean City, New Jersey, where Frank was a member of the high school basketball, baseball, and track teams and played clarinet in the school band. In his senior year, he accepted a basketball scholarship to attend the University of Delaware, where he enrolled as an engineering major. After calculus "cured" him of engineering, he switched to music education and graduated with a bachelor's degree in 1959.[1]

BEGINNINGS OF A PROFESSIONAL CAREER

Wickes's professional career began in Wilmington, Delaware, as band director at the Alexis I duPont High School. He served in that position for seven years, at the same time fulfilling his military obligation as a member of Delaware's 287th Army National Guard Band. In 1966, Wickes was admitted to graduate study at the University of Michigan in Ann Arbor. While a student there, he was a member of the Michigan Marching Band and played second chair principal clarinet in the acclaimed Michigan Symphony Band, led by the dean of college band directors, Dr. William D. Revelli. Wickes completed requirements for the master's degree in wind instrument performance in 1967.

Shortly after graduating from Michigan, Wickes took a job as band director at Fort Hunt High School in Fairfax County, Virginia. Under his direction, the Fort Hunt band flourished. It performed at the 1970 Mid-West International Band Clinic in Chicago and at the Kennedy Center in the nation's capital in 1972. That same year, the band traveled to Vienna, Austria, where it won first-place honors in an international competition. During his sixth year at Fort Hunt, Wickes accepted the band director's position at the University of Florida and in August 1973 began a seven-year tenure there.

THE ROAD TO LSU

Wickes unsuccessfully interviewed for the band director's position at the University of Iowa in 1980, where Dr. Lyle Merriman was a member of the selection committee. Merriman was later appointed dean of the LSU School of Music. When the band director's job at LSU became available, Merriman contacted Wickes and suggested that he apply. Wickes did so and received an invitation from LSU's selection committee to interview for the opening. Upon his arrival in Baton Rouge, Wickes learned that two selection committees would interview him. The first panel consisted of School of Music faculty and Dr. Huel Perkins of the university's central administration; the second was chaired by Athletic Director Paul Dietzel and included several staff members of the Athletic Department.

Each group made two specific requests of the prospective band director. The School of Music committee asked for the creation of a wind ensemble to replace the Symphonic Band as the school's premier wind instrument organization and for a change in the Tiger Band's traditional rehearsal time. The Athletic Department panel requested that the pregame performance remain unchanged and that the Golden Girls dance line continue as the featured auxiliary. Wickes pledged to honor all four requests if selected to fill the position. In 1980, Frank B. Wickes began what would turn out to be an impressive thirty-year tenure as LSU's director of bands.

PREJUDICE HAS NO PLACE

During tryouts in March 1980, for the first time since its inception in 1959, the Golden Girls dance line accepted two African American students into its ranks. Previous band director Rouse, with the support of university officials, had struggled to introduce diversity within the auxiliary ranks. Before his resignation, Rouse succeeded in planning the spring 1980 tryouts to include auditions by black students. In silent protest of the addition of black students, three members of the squad resigned, although the reason for their decision was never made public.

Rehearsals were traditionally scheduled on Thursday nights before the football games to evaluate each girl's mastery of the weekly dance routine. These sessions had come to be known as the "Thursday night cuts" since any member of the squad who

Long hours of practice for the Tiger Band, Colorguard, and Golden Girls. (LSU Band)

Golden Girls, 1980. (LSU Band)

failed to perform satisfactorily was not allowed to participate in the upcoming half-time performance. Wickes was present on the first night of the cuts. At the conclusion of the rehearsal, the two African American students were eliminated, but in Wickes's opinion unfairly so. The pair had no more errors in their routines than the others, yet they were the only ones cut. Painfully aware of the prevailing element of racial prejudice, Wickes discontinued the Thursday night cuts and retained the African American dance line members. The group accepted his decision, and the Golden Girls survived and flourished. Wickes sent a strong signal that racial prejudice had no place in LSU's Tiger Band or its auxiliary units.[2]

HONORING THE PAST

After leaving LSU in 1940, former band director Castro Carazo remained in Baton Rouge, teaching music and participating in community musical activities. During his five years as director, he composed a number of songs that he dedicated to LSU, including the ever-popular "Touchdown" and "Fight for LSU." LSU's subsequent band directors respected him, occasionally sought his counsel, and, when appropriate, seized opportunities to recognize him. Swor, for example, had invited Carazo to be guest of honor at the LSU-Auburn game on October 14, 1972, and to participate in pregame and halftime ceremonies. Attending was Senator Russell B. Long, the son of Carazo's friend Huey Long.

Wickes again recognized Carazo with a salute at the LSU-Rice game on September 26, 1981. At halftime, the band paid tribute to Carazo as it spelled out his name in huge block letters on the gridiron while serenading the fans with several of his tunes. A few weeks later, Wickes surprised Carazo with a video of the Tiger Band's halftime tribute honoring him and his many contributions to the band and the university. Carazo expressed his delight and gratitude for being remembered and so kindly honored. Just two months later, on December 28, 1981, Colonel Castro Carazo passed away.

APPEARANCE CONFLICTS

Through the years, LSU's marching band received numerous invitations to participate in parades and events on campus, around the state, throughout the country, and even internationally. The requests since 1945 had been too overwhelming to meet them all. Lovers of the band failed to understand that bandsmen were also students required to attend classes. Wickes met his first such clash on September 23, 1980, when presidential candidate Ronald Reagan visited the LSU campus to deliver a campaign speech. The event's organizers extended an invitation to Wickes for the Tiger Band to perform at Reagan's rally. Since Chancellor Paul Murrill did not instruct the faculty to authorize the release of the bandsmen from their scheduled classes and Wickes had no authority to do so, he declined the invitation.

In lieu of LSU's Tiger Band, the rally's planning committee turned to Southern University and invited the Jaguar Band, known widely since 1969 as the "Human Juke Box," to provide musical entertainment for the gathering. Southern University officials and the school's band director, Dr. Isaac Greggs, accepted the invitation but not without controversy. For their own reasons, political and otherwise, several of Southern's band members refused to participate in the rally. What's more, they did their best to prevent their band from taking the cross-town trip. Using a popular, nonviolent tactic of civil disobedience, they simply sat down in the street directly in front of the buses assigned to transport the band to LSU. After a bit of tense negotiation, the disgruntled student musicians relented and boarded the waiting vehicles. The buses rolled, and an

Carazo honored by the Tiger Band in 1981. (Photograph by Johnny Gordon)

left: Tigerama, held in the LSU Union Theater. (LSU Band)

right: Tigerama in 2008, held at the Centroplex Theater (now the River Center) in downtown Baton Rouge. (LSU Band)

hour later Southern University's band entertained Reagan and his supporters on the LSU campus.

The saga of the missing Tiger Band and its reluctant cross-town replacement did not go unnoticed. It became the focus of national attention when the story received prime-time coverage on Walter Cronkite's evening news broadcast on CBS-TV. The next morning, the LSU Band Department was deluged with telephone calls from angry alumni and others who were puzzled and dismayed that the Tiger Band had been a no-show. One of the callers went so far as to threaten Wickes's job as band director. In the fusillade was one very welcome message from Chancellor Murrill, who assured Wickes that his job was quite secure. Wickes and members of the Tiger Band who performed in the LSU Commencement Band would eventually appear at an event honoring Ronald Reagan when as United States president he accepted an honorary doctorate and was the main speaker at LSU's 1990 graduation ceremonies.

TIGERAMA

The first Tigerama concert occurred November 19, 1981, in the LSU Union Theater. It included performances by three of the School of Music's premier ensembles—the Wind Ensemble, the Jazz Band, and the Tiger Band. The Wind Ensemble, conducted by Wickes, opened the program with Leonard Bernstein's "Overture to Candide" and concluded its portion of the concert with the patriotic song "God of Our Fathers," featuring an antiphonal brass choir comprised of members of the Tiger Band. Assistant director Russell Laib then led the Jazz Band in four selections.

After intermission, the Golden Band from Tigerland made its entry onto the stage. Under the direction of drum major Greg Countryman, a music education major from Decatur, Alabama, the Tiger Band brought the audience to its feet with its "Pregame Salute," "Touchdown," and "Tiger Rag." The program included nine selections that the band had played in its 1981 halftime performances in Tiger Stadium. The first Tigerama concert ended with stirring renditions of two favorites, "Hey, Fightin' Tigers" and "Fight for LSU."

LINDA R. MOORHOUSE

In June 1983, assistant director Laib resigned and was replaced by David Morris from Tennessee. Morris, an excellent precision drill writer, served as Wickes's assistant for 1984–1985. In the summer of 1984, Linda R. Moorhouse enrolled at LSU as a graduate student with a band assistantship. Her arrival had an important impact on the Tiger Band. As a high school student, Moorhouse had learned from her band director how to edit drill charts for the marching band's shows. She had also spent summers performing with two drum and bugle corps. Because of her experience, Wickes gave Moorhouse the responsibility of managing two of the Tiger Band's auxiliary units: the Golden Girls and a new group, the Rifle Line.[3]

In the summer of 1985, when Morris resigned to return to high school teaching, Moorhouse—who had recently received her master's degree—filled the vacancy on a one-year

Linda Moorhouse directing the band during pregame. (LSU Band)

far left: Tigerettes, 1980. (LSU Band)

left: The last group of Tigerettes, 1984. (LSU Band)

The Rifle Line in action. (LSU Band)

appointment. As an instructor for the 1985–1986 term, she charted drills for the Tiger Marching Band, conducted the Symphonic Band, and supervised the auxiliaries. After successfully completing her first year, Moorhouse was named assistant director, serving in that capacity and eventually as associate director for the next twenty-four years.[4]

Wickes had found it difficult to recruit viable candidates for the band's twirling line. He announced that the Tigerettes would be phased out gradually, and ultimately disbanded at the conclusion of the 1984 football season. That year, the last remaining members of the Tigerettes graduated. Thus an old tradition was allowed to fade away with a good measure of grace and dignity.[5]

In addition to the Tiger Band's existing auxiliary units, in the fall of 1984 Moorhouse added a rifle twirling line comprised of twelve students, both males and females. The new addition of the Rifle Line was an outgrowth of then-current marching band trends that blended athleticism, jazz, showmanship, and skill. The rifle line performed with the band for three years but was disbanded at the end of the 1986 football season.[6]

FIREWORKS SINGE THE BAYLOR BAND

A potentially dangerous incident occurred at the December 27, 1985, Liberty Bowl involving the Baylor Band. To thrill the crowd, and perhaps to increase attendance, the organizers of the Liberty Bowl planned what they hoped would be a fireworks extravaganza. They constructed several boats of canvas and plywood designed to replicate U.S. naval ships of the War of 1812.

Simulating an actual naval battle, rockets were fired from the "guns" of these vessels. Instead of reaching their intended targets near the end zone, however, the rockets veered from their paths to where the Baylor Band was massed nearby. The rockets bombarded the Baylor Band with a flurry of lighted projectiles, which burst over and within their ranks. The unintended bombardment left the Baylor Band director, some of his assistants, and several of the bandsmen with their uniforms scorched and smoldering. Fortunately, no injuries occurred. As might well be imagined, the directors and students of the Baylor Band were very upset. Considering the tarnished reputation of LSU's rabidly fervent students and fans, it is within the realm of possibility that the Baylor faithful believed the debacle was no mere accident, but had been concocted by those "maniacs" from Baton Rouge!

THE ALUMNI BAND

Sponsored, planned, and hosted by the Alumni Association, the first LSU Alumni Band reunion was held September 19–20, 1986. In attendance at this historic reunion were former bandsmen, directors, and assistant directors dating as far back as 1940, including James S. Fisher, James N. Geideman, Houston C. Jenks, Oscar P. Barnes, Jr., William F. Swor, and former Tiger Band arranger John F. Edmunds. Reunion activities began with a reception in the Field House and continued the next day with breakfast at the Faculty Club, observation of the Tiger Band rehearsal in the Bernie Moore Stadium, a reunion party at the Assembly Center, and attendance at the LSU–Miami of Ohio football game. At this initial gathering, the band alumni did not play, march, or perform in any way. Plans were made and the foundation laid, however, for the next reunion the following year, during which the Alumni Band would rehearse and then perform. The Alumni Band reunion of 1986 was the first in a series extending for three decades—unbroken except for 2005, when Hurricane Katrina devastated New Orleans and much of southern Louisiana—to the present day.[7]

On September 11–12, 1987, 230 former bandsmen returned to campus to celebrate the LSU Alumni Band's second reunion. Former director Swor was chosen to lead the Alumni Band's rehearsals in preparation for its halftime performance at the LSU–California State game on September 12. Although the Tiger Band and the Alumni Band shared halftime, they did not play or march together; rather, each organization performed separately. The Tiger Band assumed a minor role, allowing the audience to

Good football makes the bandsmen happy.
(LSU Band)

top left: Former Golden Girl dance line members with the Alumni Band. (LSU Band)

top right: An LSU Alumni Band drum. (Photograph by Johnny Gordon)

right: A 2007 bandsman and . . . his alumni counterpart. (both LSU Band)

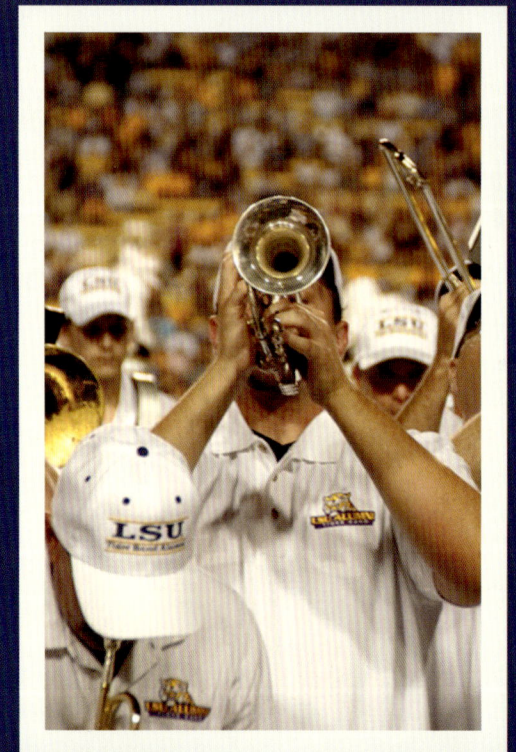

focus its attention on the Alumni Band. Its spirited renditions of LSU's songs did not disappoint the spectators, awakening a sense of nostalgia within the older Tiger fans. Although not technically perfect, the Alumni Band's performance overflowed with feeling. A constant stream of cheers and applause rewarded the alumni, cresting with a deafening standing ovation.

NO-SHOW BUSES

The first road trip on the Tiger Band's fall 1987 travel schedule was to Jackson, Mississippi, for the Tigers' game with the Ole Miss Rebels on Halloween Day. It was Joe Dean's first year as LSU's athletic director, and with his new administration came substantial personnel changes. Apparently his staff did not realize that they were responsible for arranging bus transportation for the Tiger Band's trips out of town. When the bandsmen left the rehearsal hall early that morning to load and board the buses they expected to be waiting for them, with luggage portals open and motors humming, to their surprise and shock, none were there. A hurried telephone call to the company that normally provided vehicles for the band's travels revealed that no buses had been ordered for the trip to Jackson and, worst of all, none were available. Frantic calls for help were made to other local bus companies but to no avail.

Wickes asked his bandsmen if any would be willing to drive their own vehicles to Jackson. Within minutes, 77 students volunteered to transport their fellow bandsmen to the game, by now just hours away. Soon, 280 members of the Tiger Band along with its equipment and the band's staff were on the road heading north to Jackson and the Tigers' game with archrival Ole Miss. The trip was to remain eventful. En route, a number of vehicles in the miles-long caravan stopped along the way for gas and, as might have been expected, for liquid refreshments. On the trip, five of the 77 student-driven vehicles were involved in accidents. Four of these were minor, but one car caught fire and burned. Luckily, only one minor injury was reported.

At last, the Tiger Band arrived at the stadium in Jackson. Since no provision had been made for parking spaces to accommodate nearly eighty cars and trucks, most drivers were forced to park a mile or more away from the stadium. By the middle of the game's first quarter, the band had finally gathered together and made its entrance into the stands. Undaunted, LSU's Tiger Band performed at halftime as if nothing unusual, much less catastrophic, had happened that day.

On the Tuesday following the game, Dean came to the band's rehearsal and apologized to students and staff for the transportation fiasco. He thanked the bandsmen and

To the stadium in 1983. (LSU Band)

Band in the stands, 1986. (LSU Band)

their director for overcoming adversity and for the support they gave the Tigers in their 42–13 victory over Ole Miss. Dean then gave each of the 77 drivers $150 to cover costs related to the use of their vehicles. He also promised to pay for repairs to the four cars that had been damaged along the route to Jackson and to reimburse in full the driver of the vehicle that had burned. The Tiger Band's trip to Jackson, Mississippi, on Halloween in 1987 may be recorded as one of the most unusual events of the band's long and colorful history.[8]

EVERYBODY'S ALL-AMERICAN

Everybody's All-American, a Warner Brothers movie, was filmed on the LSU campus in the spring and fall of 1987. Three up-and-coming young actors—Dennis Quaid, Jessica Lange, and Timothy Hutton—played starring roles, and dozens of students worked on the studio's production crews and served as extras. Campus sites, including Tiger Stadium, provided venues and backdrops for the story of a football icon.

To create a sense of realism and to infuse the film with the dynamic energy of young college students, Warner Brothers featured the Tiger Band in several movie sequences. In one, the bandsmen were filmed as they marched down the steps of the state capitol building, while in another, the band served as the focal point of a campus pep rally. The band figured prominently in another scene that depicted its halftime performance before a packed stadium of seventy thousand spectators.

As Wickes recalled, some interesting actions were taken by the film studio. To conceal the identity of the university depicted in the film, Warner Brothers requested that the words of several of the school's traditional cheers and songs be modified to eliminate any reference to LSU. The studio even purchased copyright privileges so that the songs could be legally incorporated into the filming. Minor alterations were made to the band's uniform; the "LSU" emblazoned on the hats and jackets was covered, and the letters "LU" appeared.

Warner Brothers chose LSU's game with Mississippi State on November 14, 1987, as the setting for the climax of the film. The studio paid the Mississippi State band $19,000 to relinquish its participation in halftime activities so that a fictitious football sequence could be filmed on the gridiron using the stadium and the huge crowd as backdrops. The Bulldog Band later used its payoff to purchase a state-of-the-art sound system for its rehearsal hall. On November 3, 1988, *Everybody's All-American* premiered in Baton Rouge at the Siegen Village Theater.

Drills on the field. (LSU Band)

PLANNING FOR THE BAND'S CENTENNIAL

In anticipation of the LSU Band's one-hundredth birthday in 1993, Wickes met with university chancellor William "Bud" Davis in the fall of 1990 to discuss plans for a series of centennial-year celebrations. Wickes proposed three ambitious projects designed to focus statewide attention on the band and its accomplishments. First, Wickes suggested the commissioning of a musician to transform a collection of school songs into a lavish medley to be named *The LSU Rhapsody*. Next, Wickes proposed taking the annual Tigerama concert on the road across the state. The traveling spectacle was to be publicized as "Tigerama on Tour." The third of the proposed celebrations was a performance at the Kennedy Center in Washington, DC, by LSU's nationally acclaimed Wind Ensemble. Invited guests would be the hundreds of LSU alumni living and working in the area. Davis, a staunch supporter of the Tiger Band, gave Wickes his approval for all three projects and pledged his administration's full support for them.

THE LSU RHAPSODY

With assurance of financial support for the band's centennial anniversary projects, Wickes contacted Academy Award–winning composer Bill Conti, an LSU alumnus and a former bandsman. Because of prior commitments, Conti was unable to accept the commission to create *The LSU Rhapsody*. He did, however, give Wickes the names of two composers he felt were capable of accomplishing the task: Bruce Healey and Ken Whitcomb, both employed at the time by Disney Studios. Conti facilitated Wickes's first telephone contact with Healey and Whitcomb, during which the three discussed the project at length. The composers asked myriad questions about the instrumentation and capabilities of the Wind Ensemble. Apparently satisfied with Wickes's responses, they accepted the commission to create a medley of LSU songs. *The LSU Rhapsody* is a special tribute to LSU, intertwining six of the university's most famous songs into one work of, as Wickes put it, "rich harmonies and spirited melodies." The songs, in order of presentation in the rhapsody, are "Touchdown for LSU," "Darling of LSU," "Hey, Fightin' Tigers," "LSU Alma Mater," "Fight for LSU," and "Tiger Rag."

TIGERAMA ON TOUR

Tigerama on Tour was a massive undertaking that included the Wind Ensemble, the Jazz Ensemble, and the Tiger Band, along with the Golden Girls, the Colorguard, and the student tiger mascot. Two concert tours showcased Tigerama in seven Louisiana cities and in Houston, home to the second largest number of LSU alumni outside of Baton Rouge. The tour of April 10–14, 1991, took Tigerama to Shreveport, Monroe, Houma, Lake Charles, and Chalmette. During the Shreveport concert, the Wind Ensemble gave the premiere performance of the newly composed *LSU Rhapsody*. One year later, Tigerama again went on the road. In its second tour, April concerts were given in Houston, Thibodaux, and Lafayette. Wickes announced that Tigerama on Tour served as a preliminary celebration for the LSU Band's one-hundredth-anniversary observance in 1993. The Tiger Marching Band performance ended each concert with the most popular LSU songs: "Hey, Fightin' Tigers" and the John Edmunds arrangement of "Fight for LSU."[9]

Wickes debuted *The LSU Rhapsody* on campus during a Wind Ensemble concert after the return from Tigerama on Tour. Later in 2008, Bill Conti visited LSU and conducted the successful medley whose composition he had facilitated.

Wickes with the band's guest Bill Conti in 2008. (LSU Band)

CENTENNIAL CELEBRATIONS

Few Tiger faithful are aware that two of LSU's most popular and revered institutions share a common heritage: both the band and the football team were founded in 1893. That spring, eleven cadets gathered to form a brass band for their alma mater, and at about the same time a handful of student athletes volunteered to play on their school's first football team. To commemorate these significant events in the university's history and to celebrate their centennial anniversary, the Alumni Band and the Tiger Band joined forces to perform together at halftime of the LSU-Tulane football game on November 20, 1993. The extravaganza concluded with a very special surprise for the Tiger Stadium crowd of 58,000 spectators.

Dawson Corley, former Tiger bandsman and creator of the Louisiana State Archives' *100 Golden Years* historical exhibition, arranged for Cy Coleman, composer of "Hey, Look Me Over," to guest-conduct at a halftime performance. In 1962 Coleman's song was adapted for LSU's exclusive use. New words were written, the new title "Hey, Fightin' Tigers" was invented, and a rousing arrangement of the song was created for the Tiger Band. The halftime performance of the combined Alumni and Tiger Bands playing "Hey, Fightin' Tigers," conducted by Coleman, was a fitting climax to the centennial anniversary celebrations honoring the Golden Band from Tigerland and the LSU Tiger football team.

As part of the Golden Centennial celebrations, the Wind Ensemble was featured in performance at the John F. Kennedy Center for the Performing Arts on February 9, 1994. The national capital was chosen because the presence of a large contingent of LSU alumni and Louisiana dignitaries in the area portended an enthusiastic audience and reconnected the Louisianans with LSU. To lend a touch of Louisiana hospitality to the occasion, Chancellor Davis hosted a pre-concert reception for the guests. Although an ice storm adversely affected attendance, the concert was a musical and artistic success for LSU and Louisiana.[10]

FALL FEST

LSU's first Fall Fest was held on Friday, September 2, 1994. The event was conceived as a welcome-back-to-campus festivity for students and as an oversized pep rally designed to kick off the football

Joint Tiger Band and Alumni Band. (Photograph by Johnny Gordon)

season, promote school spirit, and spark student enthusiasm for the Tigers' opening football game with Texas A&M on the next day. The rally featured the cheerleaders, members of the football coaching staff, and the Tiger Band, along with the band's Colorguard and Golden Girls. Its venue—the enclosed confines of the university quadrangle—magnified the sound of the band and the cheers of hundreds of students who were waiting for class, passing between classes, or cutting class. Spirits ran high, perhaps to the chagrin of some professors who no doubt found it disconcerting to attempt to compete with the commotion just outside the classroom doors. Fall Fest became an annual campus event featuring the Tiger Band.

EXPANDED DUTIES

After a successful one-year appointment as assistant band director, Linda Moorhouse joined the School of Music faculty and assumed the position of assistant director on an ongoing basis. Born in Minneapolis in 1960, Moorhouse moved with her family to Seattle and later to Florida, where her father worked with the National Aeronautics and Space Administration (NASA). She studied clarinet and played in the Gainesville High School marching band. An influential band director there taught the talented student to chart drills for the marching band, a rare opportunity for a high school bandsman. While pursuing the master's degree that she completed at LSU in 1985, Moorhouse oversaw the auxiliary units and charted the marching band programs. After becoming assistant band director, she conducted the Symphonic Band and the Symphonic Winds, charted all movements of the Tiger Band's performances, instituted three summer camps, and supervised auditions for the band and auxiliaries. Her colleagues stated that she was focused, proficient, and a tireless worker. Students found her ability to communicate with them extremely helpful in times of difficulties.[11]

After a two-year leave of absence, 1993–1995, to pursue doctoral studies in music at the University of Washington, Moorhouse returned to LSU to resume her duties in the Band Department. John La Cognata was hired to serve as assistant band director during Moorhouse's two-year leave. In 1998, Moorhouse was granted a second leave of absence to complete requirements for the doctorate. Roy M. King, who had recently completed a master's in music education at LSU, was appointed temporary assistant director. With his responsibilities steadily escalating, Wickes requested funding from LSU athletic director Joe Dean to hire another permanent assistant. Dean provided funds, and King was selected to become Wickes's second assistant, beginning in fall 1999.

At Moorhouse's request, Wickes allowed her to assume expanded responsibility for the Tiger Band and its two auxiliary units.

below: Linda Moorhouse walks with the band to the game in a downpour. (LSU Band)

facing page: Drums at Fall Fest. (Photograph by Rachel Saltzberg)

Golden Girls under supervision of Moorhouse. (Photograph by Rachel Saltzberg)

With nearly total control of the entire 325-member organization, she closely supervised the Golden Girls and the Colorguard, wrote and rehearsed the band's halftime drills, and conducted its music and marching rehearsals. Moorhouse conducted pregame performances, and as was the tradition, drum majors conducted the half-time shows. Wickes's trust in Moorhouse proved to be well placed. In 1997 the Tiger Band was voted the number one marching band in the Southeastern Conference, and in September 2002, it won the prestigious Sudler Trophy, the greatest honor a university marching band can receive. In 1998, Moorhouse was promoted to associate band director.

From 1995 until his retirement in 2010, Wickes served faithfully as a self-relegated marching band assistant to Moorhouse, seldom missing a Tiger Band rehearsal. Taking his place on the practice field with King while Moorhouse led the practices, he constantly moved between and among his bandsmen, offering help wherever needed. In the annals of university bands, it is probable that such a reversal of roles seldom, if ever, has worked so well and been so successful.

The Colorguard was also supervised by Moorhouse. (Photograph by Rachel Saltzberg)

ROCK STARS

On October 11, 1997, the LSU Tigers hosted the number one Florida Gators in a game long remembered. LSU defeated Florida by a score of 28–21, and as the game ended, thousands of Tiger students and fans stampeded onto the field. Pandemonium erupted. Within minutes, the goalposts were torn down and turf was ripped up. All the while, the Tiger Band, safe in its seats high above the melee, played on, contributing to the frenzy on the field. Finally, as the stadium began to empty, the jubilant students crowded together in one massive throng below and in front of the band, and the bandsmen became the object of their cheers. The postgame concert continued for some time, until the chants ebbed and the stadium lights dimmed. At last, the band began its exit, bringing down the curtain on an unforgettable night in Tiger Stadium. For one brief moment the student musicians, the dancers, and the flag bearers had all been made to feel like rock stars, and to many of their fellow students, they were indeed!

TIGER BAND VOTED BEST IN SEC

Also in 1997, Waylon T. Rice, a reporter for the *Northwest Arkansas Times,* polled all twelve of the Southeastern Conference marching band directors and asked them to rank the top six bands, excluding their own. Ten responded to Rice's request. The vote was unanimous. All of the responding directors selected the Golden Band from Tigerland as the SEC's number one marching band.

left: The 325-member band. (LSU Band)

right: Drums in their stadium seats. (Photograph by Rachel Saltzberg)

facing page: The Tiger Band waits to step onto the field. (Photograph by Rachel Saltzberg)

According to Athletic Director Dean, the poll only confirmed what LSU fans had always known, that their Tiger Marching Band was the grandest band in all the land. "It's nice of the band directors to say the things they did," said Wickes. "Of course, there's no way to really know who has the best band because you can't see them all. But the fact that the poll was unanimous in our favor makes it very special."

LSU'S FEMALE DRUM MAJORS

KRISTIE SMITH

On the night of September 4, 1999, eighty thousand Tiger football fans witnessed history in the making. Although for a brief time during World War II two drum majorettes led the band, for the first time a female drum major led LSU's Golden Band from Tigerland onto the gridiron. Kristie Smith, an LSU senior majoring in music education and a native of Jennings, Louisiana, had earned the honor. After a grueling weekend of tryouts and interviews, she was chosen from a pool of eleven applicants to lead the 325-member Tiger Band in the 1999 football season.

Writing in the *Jennings Daily News,* on September 26, 1999, Brent Mitchell stated: "So the next time you're in Death Valley and the Tigers make a touchdown, go ahead and join in the cheers emanating from the stadium. And as you pump your arm forward and backward while chanting at the top of your lungs, realize that a local girl is at the root of all that excitement."[12]

MINDY HEBERT

A long, taxing audition of nearly eight hours resulted in the selection of Mindy Hebert as drum major of the Tiger Band for the 2000 football season. The second female drum major at LSU, she followed her best friend, Kristie Smith, in winning that coveted position. For Mindy, leading the Golden Band from Tigerland was a dream come true. A native of Walker, Louisiana, Mindy played trumpet in her high school band and served as its drum major. After graduation, she enrolled at LSU and began studies in music education, with hopes of one day becoming a band director. Not until 2014 would a third woman drum major, Mary Bahlinger from Mandeville, Louisiana, lead the Tiger Band.

A MUSICAL TRIBUTE TO THE VICTIMS OF 9/11

The terrorist attacks of September 11, 2001, shocked and appalled the nation but failed to intimidate its citizens. In part because of the tragedy, LSU's first home football game of the 2001 season was delayed until October 6. The Tiger Band closed its halftime performance on that day with a tribute to the thousands of Americans who died in New York, at the Pentagon, and in Pennsylvania. In reverence to the memory of their fallen countrymen, the bandsmen knelt and removed their hats. The bare-headed bandsmen then played a moving rendition of "Amazing Grace."

As the strains of the music floated high in the air, the ninety-two thousand spectators fell into total silence. At that moment there were few dry eyes on the field or in the stands. LSU's Golden Band from Tigerland seemed to be blessed with a touch of

left: The Colorguard in Tigerama at the Maravich Assembly Center. (LSU Band)

right: Honoring the fallen of 9/11, with hats on the ground. (Photograph by Rachel Saltzberg)

magic. In the opinions of many of those present, the sounds produced by the band in that singular performance may have been more beautiful than any ever before heard in Tiger Stadium. All who witnessed this amazing tribute became as one in spirit and resolve.

TIGER BANDSMEN "PLAY" FOOTBALL

LSU's football game with Auburn in the 2001 season was to have been played on September 15, but because of the terrorist attacks of 9/11, the game was rescheduled for December 1. As the Tiger Band was concluding its halftime performance, Auburn's kicking team was sent out of the dressing room to warm up. When the band began its exit maneuver, two Auburn kickers blocked the paths of several bandsmen. As a tuba player approached one of the Auburn kickers, a collision seemed imminent. At that instant, the Auburn player took a swing at the bandsman but was knocked off balance by one of the band's baritone players who had come to the aid of his friend and fellow musician. Riveted by the fracas unfolding on the field, the crowd in the south end zone erupted in wild cheers in support of the two LSU bandsmen. Auburn lost the game by a score of 27–14. The sports commentator calling the game for ESPN later remarked, "Auburn had a terrible time at LSU. Not only could they not beat the Tiger football team, they couldn't beat the Tiger Band, either!"

The next day ESPN reported the halftime fiasco, and it soon came to the attention of Tommy Tuberville, Auburn's coach. After a bit of fact finding, he telephoned Wickes and apologized for his players' poor conduct. Tuberville wrote a letter of apology, which Wickes later read to the entire band, and the incident reached a satisfactory conclusion.

THE SUDLER TROPHY

The John Philip Sousa Foundation administers the annual awarding of the Sudler Trophy, named for Louis and Virginia Sudler, whose keen interest in bands and band music inspired the creation of the award in 1983. Regarded as the highest honor a university marching band can receive, the Sudler is known as the "Heisman Trophy" of

Balloons fall on the Tiger Band and players as they enter through the band's tunnel. (LSU Band)

A bandsman's view from the tunnel.
(Photograph by Rachel Saltzberg)

the collegiate band world. In December 2001, officials of the Sousa Foundation notified Wickes, Moorhouse, and King that LSU's Tiger Band had been selected to receive the prestigious prize.

As stated by the Sousa Foundation, "The purpose of the Sudler Trophy is to identify and recognize collegiate marching bands of particular excellence, which have made outstanding contributions to the American way of life. The Sudler Trophy is awarded annually to a college or university marching band which has demonstrated the highest musical standards and innovative marching routines and ideas, and which has made important contributions to the advancement of the performance standards of college marching bands over a period of years."[13]

The Sousa Foundation bases its selection process on a comprehensive survey sent to every marching band director at four-year schools with football programs regulated by the NCAA. Each director may nominate three university bands worthy of the Sudler Trophy. The foundation's award committee then creates a final ballot, from which the directors select the winner.

In a special ceremony in Tiger Stadium on September 14, 2002, officials of the Sousa Foundation presented the Sudler Trophy to the Tiger Band and its directors at halftime of the LSU–Miami of Ohio football game. The occasion marked the second time in its history that the LSU Band has been honored as the nation's best.

COLLEGE BAND CONTEST

In 2008, ESPN, Paramount Pictures, and Lucasfilm sponsored the "Indiana Jones Battle of the Bands" music video contest to promote the fourth film in the Indiana Jones series. Contest organizers limited the competition to bands whose football teams were ranked in the top ten of the 2008 BCS preseason poll. At the time, the Tiger football team ranked number six nationally; therefore, the LSU Band was invited to enter the contest. After consulting with the bandsmen, directors Wickes, Moorhouse, and King accepted the challenge.

One of the contest guidelines required that each of the competing bands play the title theme from *Raiders of the Lost Ark,* the 1981 film that began the series, while executing its own unique marching drill. ESPN camera crews filmed the performances of the bands on their schools' campuses for Internet presentation. The band garnering the most votes for its rendition of the tune and its accompanying marching routine would be declared the winner. Fans were not limited to one vote but could vote multiple times; surely many did.

Moorhouse asked the Athletic Department to allow the band to use the indoor football practice facility for rehearsing and filming its music video. To prepare the band's various sections, the bandsmen worked after classes and on weekends, designing and perfecting routines to be performed to the strains of the *Raiders* theme. Special costumes were created for the Golden Girls. Even the student tiger mascot got into the act and dressed to resemble Indiana Jones with his wide-brimmed safari hat.

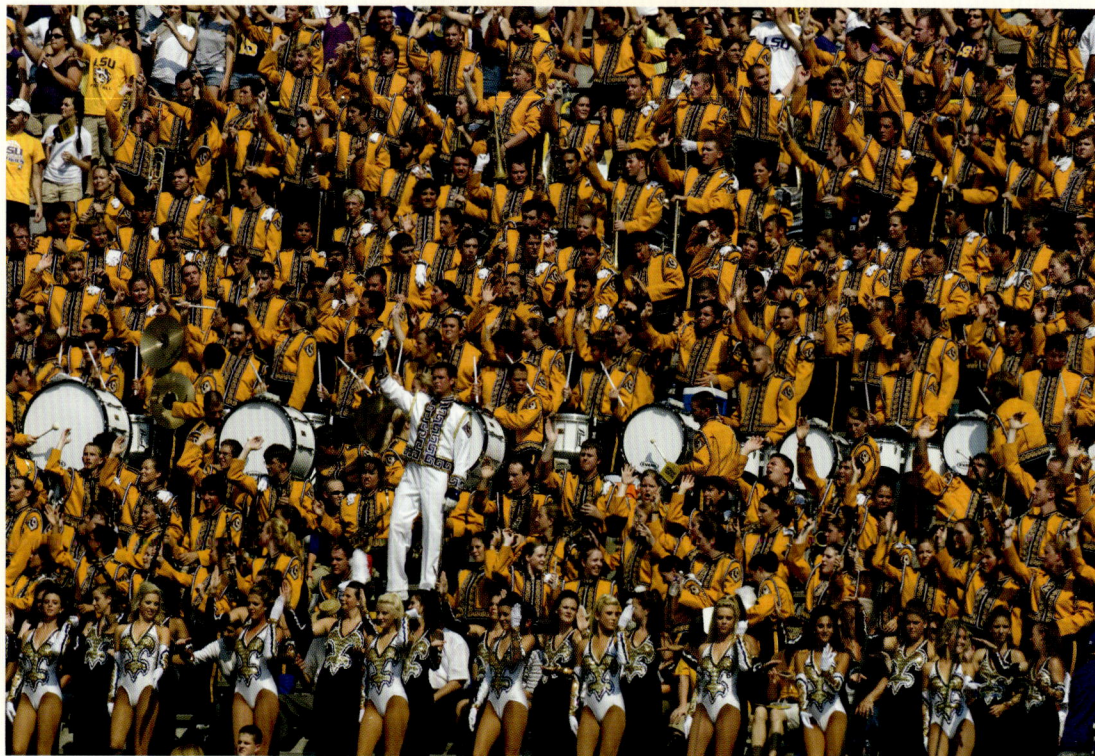

Band in the stands, 2007. (Photograph by Rachel Saltzberg)

left: On the way to the stadium in the rain for the Tiger Band's induction into the Louisiana Music Hall of Fame. (Photograph by Rachel Saltzberg)

right: Band's salute to the Louisiana Music Hall of Fame. (LSU Band)

Moorhouse persuaded Coach Les Miles to make a cameo appearance in the video. Surrounded by the Golden Girls, he pointed menacingly at the camera with his index finger and clenched fist and repeated his then-famous remark, as acerbic as when first delivered on ESPN television a year or so earlier: "Have a nice day!" No one can be sure, but Miles's cameo may well have tipped the scale in favor of the Tiger Band.

When the votes were counted, LSU tallied more than seventy-five thousand and was declared winner. For its victory, the band received an award of $25,000, which paled in comparison with the public relations bonanza its performance earned for the university.

THE LOUISIANA MUSIC HALL OF FAME

On September 12, 2009, the Golden Band from Tigerland was inducted into the Louisiana Music Hall of Fame. Nominated by former bandsman Del Moon, it was the first college marching band in Louisiana to be so honored. On a rainy Saturday night at halftime of the LSU-Vanderbilt football game, officials of the Louisiana Music Hall of Fame presented the award to the band and its directors, Wickes, Moorhouse, and King, before ninety-two thousand spectators.

The day before, honored guests Nina Carazo Snapp, granddaughter of former LSU band director Castro Carazo, and Kay Long, granddaughter of former Louisiana governor Huey P. Long, attended a special ceremony at the Lod Cook Alumni Center, along with the Tiger Band. Snapp and Long represented their famous grandfathers' induction into the newly established Songwriters Division of the Louisiana Music Hall of Fame.

The Hall of Fame award announcement stated: "The distinction is just the latest in a long series of singular achievements that easily demonstrate that it has earned the honor. That doesn't even account for the way the Tiger Band is weaved into LA history: no other school band was founded by a future governor, has had fight songs written by another governor, or benefited from having a famed jazz orchestra leader as its bandmaster. Few other college bands are as integral to the identity and lore of their athletic programs and campus culture. Finally, few other band programs have produced as many musicians, music educators and famed alumni in the music world."[14]

GOLDEN GIRLS' FIFTIETH ANNIVERSARY

Since Tom Tyra created the popular Golden Girls dance line in 1959, approximately eight hundred LSU women, selected for their beauty, poise, charm, grace, and dancing ability, have claimed membership. Almost two hundred of them returned to campus on October 31, 2009, to celebrate the fifty-year reunion of the dance line and to perform with the Alumni Band at halftime of the LSU-Tulane football game. Logistically, it was hard to get all two hundred on the field and also to fashion a costume that both a twenty-year-old and a seventy-year-old could flatteringly wear as they performed traditional Golden Girls routines. Alumna Carol Hoffpauir Hebert, 1967–1969, recalled the time when the Tiger Band marched in Atlanta's Peach Bowl parade for two miles in freezing weather.

left: The Golden Girls in 1984. (LSU Band)

right: The Golden Girls in 1990. (LSU Band)

Worse was walking two miles back to the hotel with no coat. "Then," Hebert said, "it had the nerve to rain at the game." Another member of the Golden Girls, Sally Burtner Bourgeois, 1976–1978, remembered "how we could laugh at ourselves in adverse situations; turning blue in freezing temperatures, or dancing to Christmas music in a downpour and 80-degree weather."[15]

CAPITAL ONE BOWL, 2010

The deluge on the morning of the LSU–Penn State bowl game in 2010 further loosened recently added field sod that had already been rain soaked for over three weeks. During the Tiger Band's pregame entrance onto the field, band members sank into the muddy surface, some losing shoes that became stuck in the muck, creating a very uneven appearance of the pregame lines throughout the show. Before halftime, stadium officials notified both bands that there would be no marching shows on the field at the half. As an alternative, the bands were allowed to walk onto the field, line up in a concert formation, and play their shows facing their fans at midfield. This was to be the final game-day memory for director of bands Frank B. Wickes as he concluded his tenure with the Golden Band from Tigerland.

For three decades, Wickes served LSU and the Golden Band from Tigerland with professional excellence, integrity, and honor. Judged by the national recognition, accolades, and awards that the Tiger Band received under his direction, this was the most productive period in its history. Wickes retired in June 2010.

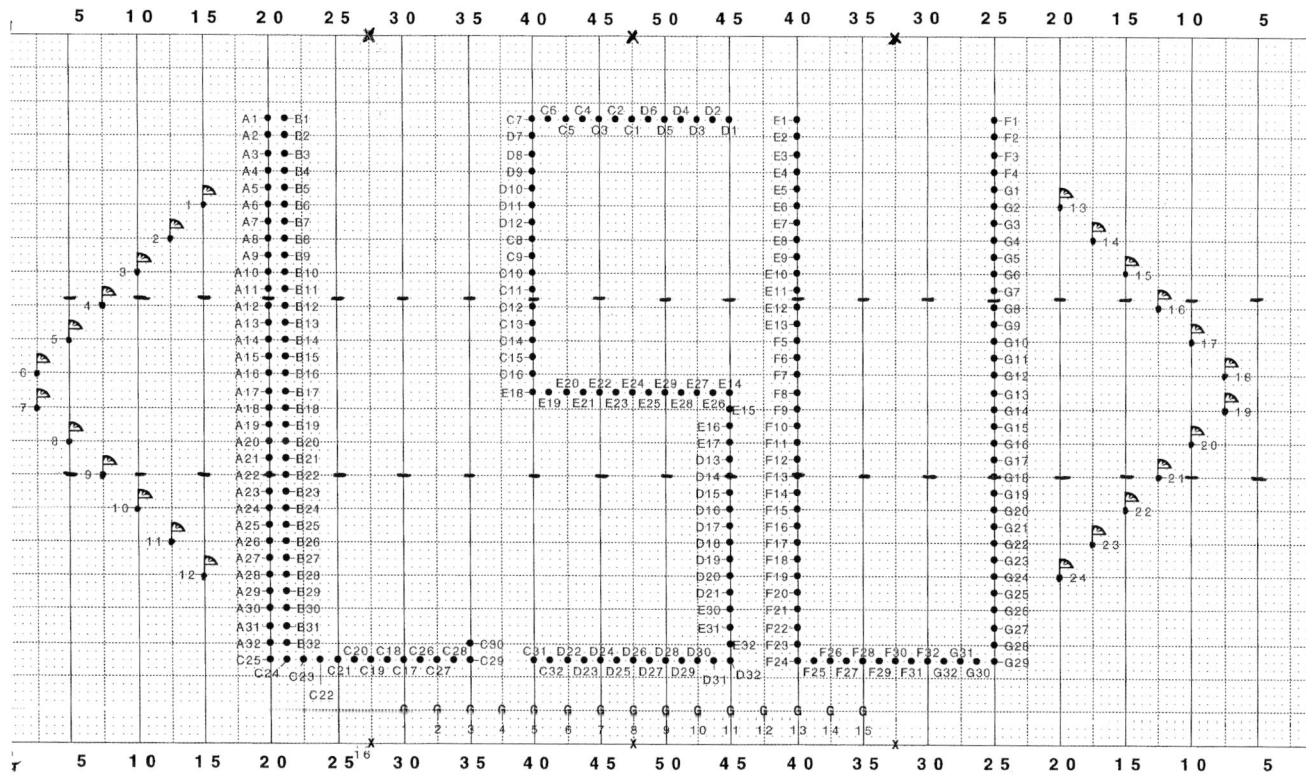

Marching band computer chart for LSU pregame, 2001. (LSU Band)

The Golden Girls in 2010. (Photograph by Rachel Saltzberg)

Frank B. Wickes led the Golden Band from Tigerland for thirty years.
(Photograph by Rachel Saltzberg)

The tradition continues into the stadium.
(Photograph by Rachel Saltzberg)

8

THE TRADITION CONTINUES

Well over a century has passed since two cadets of the Ole War Skule decided to create a brass band for their alma mater. With the passage of time and because of the hard work and dedication of many, the dream of Wylie Barrow and Ruffin Pleasant flourished and lives today as LSU's beloved Golden Band from Tigerland.

In three separate epochs, the LSU Band reached the heights of national acclaim and experienced golden ages—under directors Castro Carazo in the 1930s, William F. Swor in the 1970s, and Frank B. Wickes in the first decade of the twenty-first century. Under a new director, talented and charismatic, a fourth golden age is sure to come. The tradition continues!

ROY M. KING

Roy M. King received a bachelor of music education degree and a master of music degree in wind conducting from LSU. In 1998, after fourteen years as a high school band director in Georgia, Kentucky, Louisiana, and Florida, King accepted an appointment as assistant director of bands at LSU. In 2010, after Frank Wickes retired and Linda Moorhouse joined the University of Illinois School of Music faculty, King became director of athletic bands at LSU. In that capacity, he directed the 325-member Tiger Band and the Bengal Brass Basketball Band. Additionally, he supervised the activities of all other university athletic bands. As a faculty member in the School of Music, King also taught undergraduate courses in wind instrument conducting and marching band techniques.

THE NEW TIGER BAND HALL

Regrettably, the Band Hall was constructed in 1959 with one unforeseen flaw, its size. Within little more than a decade, the Tiger Band outgrew the facility. Nearly forty years would pass before the LSU Band acquired an adequate indoor practice place.

State senator Robert Adley spearheaded the 2007 allocation of five million dollars of the state's construction budget for planning, design, and construction of a modern, updated band complex. However, the money from the state had to be matched dollar for dollar by LSU. A steering committee was appointed to lead the effort to raise private funds for the new band hall. The Athletic Department committed four million dollars to the project. Private donors contributed the balance, thus fulfilling LSU's obligation.[1]

Finally, on June 14, 2010, construction began on the new band hall. One year later, the Tiger Band moved into its new, permanent home. The modern complex offers eighteen thousand square feet of usable space under one roof. The heart of the building, the rehearsal hall, is the size of a basketball court and comfortably accommodates the band's 325 members, with ample space for future increases.

STEPHEN LEE KOIVISTO, BAND INSTRUMENT REPAIR TECHNICIAN

In the tradition established by former band instrument technicians "Mr. G." and Mark Vandermark, and aided by a small crew of students, Stephen Lee Koivisto spends the summer months repairing, removing scratches and dents, and polishing a vast array of

Roy King conducting pregame. (Photograph by Rachel Saltzberg)

instruments. The responsibilities of repairing and maintaining hundreds of the School of Music's wind, string, and percussion instruments, as well as the Tiger Band's inventory of school-owned instruments, are staggering. Koivisto also teaches a class in instrument repair.

A native of Jacksonville, Florida, Koivisto attended the Victory Christian Academy there. He played clarinet in the school band and served as its drum major in his sophomore year. He earned a bachelor of music degree from Georgia Southern University and a master of music degree in clarinet performance at the University of Southern Mississippi. An accomplished clarinetist, Koivisto has played with the Charlotte Symphony, the South Carolina Philharmonic, and the Charleston Symphony.

As a youngster, Koivisto was blessed with an attraction to, and a knack for, all things mechanical. On his first day of seventh-grade beginning band, he took his clarinet home. Without hesitation, he took it apart, key by key, and, unassisted, correctly reassembled the complex woodwind instrument. This ability led Koivisto to a professional career in instrument repair, beginning at the King Band Instrument Repair Company of DeKalb, Georgia; next as shop manager with the Mississippi Music Company of Hattiesburg; and eventually at his own company, Palmetto Instrument Repair in Columbia, South Carolina. Fifteen years later, in 2012, Koivisto accepted his current position in the LSU Band Department.[2]

Each summer, Koivisto prepares the band's instruments for the upcoming football season. Just in time for preseason rehearsals in August, all is ready. Looking shiny and new, the instruments await the arrival of the bandsmen who will play them for the duration of football season. When the Tiger Band takes the field at each season's first

Steve Koivisto repairs the band instruments when and wherever needed: in the shop, on the field, or at Alumni Band rehearsals. (Photographs courtesy of Steve Koivisto)

pregame, at that moment, perhaps more than any other, Koivisto knows he's done his job.

DRUM MAJOR MARY BAHLINGER

In May 2014, Mary Elizabeth Bahlinger was named the Tiger Band's drum major for the 2014 football season. Just the third female member to serve the band in that capacity since its founding in 1893 and the first since 2000, Mary evinces the determination and hard work needed to become the Tiger Band's drum major, male or female. The tryouts for drum major have long been a two-day affair demanding outstanding marching, conducting, and mace abilities. Like her predecessors, Mary survived the day-one cuts and at the conclusion of the second day of competition was chosen Tiger Band drum major.

Mary's words immediately before stepping out onto the field in front of the Tiger Band at pregame for her first appearance as drum major could perhaps have been spoken by all past and future drum majors: "Walking into Reliant Stadium before the LSU-Wisconsin game in Houston, I imagined I would be nervous, very nervous as Pregame approached. But I realized that even though the setting was different from that of our own practice field at home and of Tiger Stadium, the actual performance of Pregame was no different, it was exactly the same as what I had been practicing and preparing for months."[3]

above: **Bahlinger with number one fan Mike the Tiger. (Photograph by Rachel Saltzberg)**

facing page: **Mary Bahlinger, drum major. (Photograph by Rachel Saltzberg)**

TIGERAMA

The annual Tigerama concert has evolved into one of the most anticipated and popular musical events on the LSU campus. Year by year, the band's Tigerama audiences grew and the requests for tickets increased, far exceeding the seating capacity of the university's Union Theater. To accommodate the increasing crowds, Tigerama moved to the Maravich Assembly Center in 2003. It has been staged in that venue ever since, except for two engagements at Baton Rouge's River Center in 2009 and 2010.

In keeping with tradition, the concert's original format has remained for the most part unchanged. A brief performance by the combined Wind Ensemble and Symphonic Winds precedes the Tiger Band's appearance, which concludes the concert with rousing renditions of LSU's school songs. As always, the audience erupts in applause and cheers, honoring the Golden Band from Tigerland with foot-stomping standing ovations.

The fans look forward to the Golden Girls' dance routines on the 50-yard line. (Photograph by Rachel Saltzberg)

AMBASSADORS OF DANCE AND GOODWILL

In February 2011, LSU's popular dance teams, the Golden Girls and the Tiger Girls, accompanied by the student tiger mascot, traveled halfway around the world to perform in the Cathay Pacific International New Year Night Parade in Hong Kong.[4] This spectacular event, sponsored by Hong Kong's tourism board, rings in the Chinese New Year, the most celebrated of all Chinese holidays.

The Tiger Girls perform at the LSU men's and women's home basketball games and at some baseball games. Unlike the Golden Girls, they are not a unit of the Tiger Band but a unit of the spirit teams in the Athletic Department. The Hong Kong tourism board contacted Pauline Zernott, LSU spirit coordinator and director of the Tiger Girls, to express interest in a performance by an LSU dance team of approximately thirty members. To create an ensemble of that size, Zernott combined her dancers with the Golden Girls. For the students, staff, and chaperones, traveling to Hong Kong to celebrate the Chinese New Year presented an opportunity of a lifetime. The tourism board provided all travel costs. The trip constituted a series of firsts: first trip to Hong Kong for many; first time an LSU group was invited to take part in the Cathay parade; and first time the Tiger Girls and Golden Girls officially performed together in public.

LSU's combined dance teams performed in the parade at spectator stands spaced along the march route. They also appeared at the Hong Kong Cultural Center Piazza and at several other venues in the city. In touring the countryside, the entourage ventured to the small village of Tai Po Lam Tsuen. The villagers received the dancers and Mike the mascot with much glee and enthusiasm. The costumed Mike stole the show with his unique renditions of "Thriller" and "Quick Change."

PURPLE AND GOLD WITH A TOUCH OF GREEN

The LSU Band had traveled throughout Louisiana and to other states as far distant as New York, but until the Hong Kong trip, not even its auxiliary units had ever left American shores to visit a foreign land. That opportunity presented itself again when Dublin, Ireland's mayor extended an official invitation to the Tiger Band to march in the city's annual St. Patrick's Day Parade for 2014. On behalf of 325 bandsmen and with the approval of LSU's administration, band director King accepted the mayor's offer. Thousands of miles to the east and far from home, the Golden Band from Tigerland would march and play in the grandest of St. Patrick's Day parades.

On the morning of March 14, 2014, the bandsmen, accompanied by twenty-five staff and guests, boarded various flights in New Orleans, Houston, and Atlanta, all of them bound for Ireland. LSU's president and chancellor, F. King Alexander, and former director of bands Frank Wickes accompanied the band as honored guests. Because many of the band's instruments could not be accommodated by the airlines, United Parcel Service (UPS) was hired to transport them to Dublin several weeks prior to the parade. As soon as King stepped off the plane, he headed straight to the warehouse where the instruments had been temporarily stored to assure himself they were safe and in good condition.

King and his staff devised a plan to raise funds from several divergent sources for the projected $750,000 cost of the trip. Proceeds from the annual Tigerama concert and silent auction were earmarked for the trip, as were donations from band supporters. In lieu of the bandsmen's service award stipends, the Athletic Department contributed

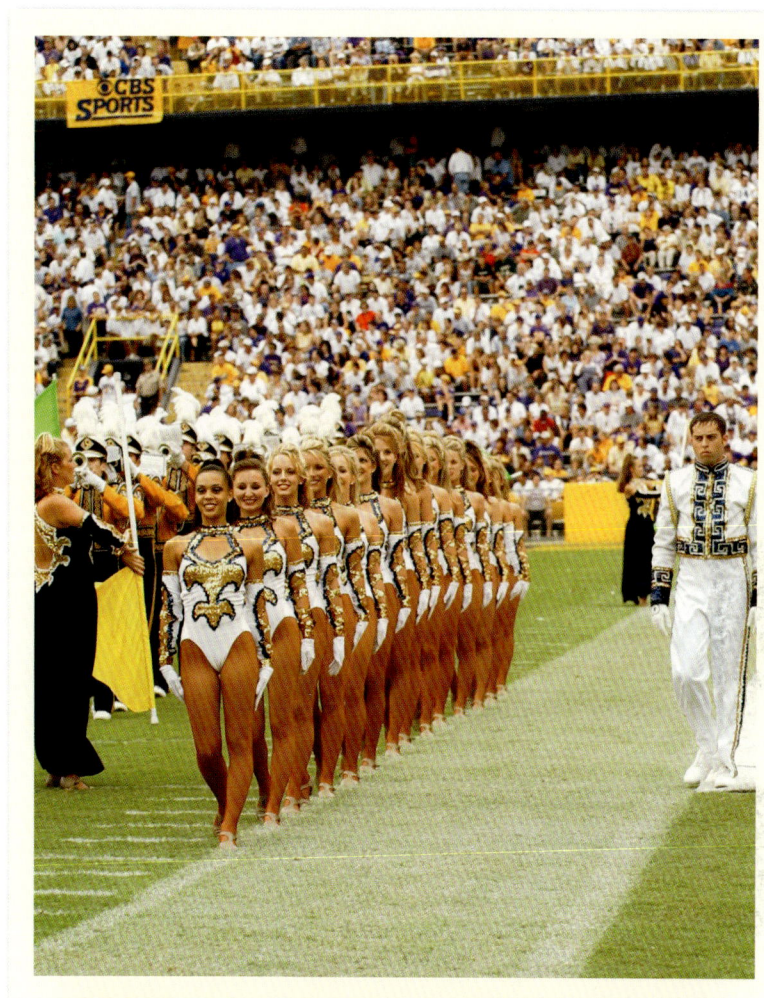

The quality of the Golden Girls' routines took them to China. (LSU Band)

Band performing in Ireland parade. (Photographs by Rachel Saltzberg)

$350,000 to the cause. Despite these efforts, funds fell short of the goal by $100,000. Unexpectedly, an LSU alumnus and former letterman on Coach Charles McClendon's 1977 football squad saved the day. Ralph C. McIngvale, a successful Houston businessman, made a gift of $100,000 to the Tiger Band, which thus reached its goal.[5]

The Tiger Band was the largest marching contingent in the St. Patrick's Day Parade and, by all accounts, a favorite of the thousands of spectators who lined the parade route. Via local Baton Rouge television, the band's performance touched the hearts of viewers at home as it represented LSU, Louisiana, and America.

FOOTBALL SATURDAY . . . A DAY WITH THE TIGER BAND

It begins with crowded interstate highways and city streets jammed with vehicles, bumper to bumper, edging slowly to a common destination. On this game day as on all others when the Tigers play at home, the campus is transformed into the freakiest, funkiest, and most frenzied venue in all of college football. Death Valley and its environs host the biggest, noisiest tailgate party anywhere in America. This is game day at LSU!

As the hours roll by and game time approaches, excitement and revelry intensify, gradually giving way to what can only be described as a state of acute pandemonium. And finally, far off in the distance, the faint sounds of approaching drums. Welcome to "Football Saturday and a Day with the Tiger Band"!

A DAY WITH THE TIGER BAND

Photographs by Rachel Saltzberg

APPENDIX

LSU BAND DIRECTORS AND DATES OF TENURE

Ruffin G. Pleasant	Fall 1893–Spring 1896; Fall 1897–Spring 1898
W. B. Clarke	Spring 1896–Fall 1897; Spring 1906–Spring 1915
Charles A. Kellogg	Fall 1898–Spring 1903
Frank E. Miller	Fall 1903–Fall 1904
D. P. West	Fall 1904–Spring 1906
Henry W. Stopher	Fall 1915–Spring 1918
Frank T. Guilbeau	Spring 1918–December 1930
Alfred W. Wickboldt	December 1930–December 1934
Castro Carazo	January 1935–August 1940
Arthur M. Culpepper	August 1940–Spring 1942
James S. Fisher	July 1942–January 1944
William E. Koogler	January 1944–October 1944
Andrew J. McMullen	October 1944–September 1945
Llewellyn Bruce Jones	September 1945–July 1958
Thomas N. Tyra	August 1958–June 1964
William F. Swor	Fall 1964–June 1977
Nicholas M. Rouse	June 1977–Spring 1980
Frank B. Wickes	Fall 1980–Spring 2010
Roy M. King	Fall 2010–Spring 2016

NOTES

1. FROM HUMBLE BEGINNINGS, 1893–1930

1. Louisiana State University, Baton Rouge, *Catalog, 1899–1900,* 68; *Catalog, Fall 1903–Spring 1904,* 69.

2. LSU, *Catalog, Fall 1902–Spring 1903,* 76.

3. *Baton Rouge Morning Advocate,* October 30, 1942.

4. Louisiana State University, Baton Rouge, *Reveille,* October 17, 1907, February 28, December 4, 1908; *Advocate,* February 22, 1908.

5. *Reveille,* April 19, 1919; *Memphis Commercial Appeal,* www.historic-Memphis.com.

6. *Baton Rouge State Times,* December 19, 1927.

7. LSU, *Catalog, Fall 1915–Spring 1916,* 224; *Catalog, Fall 1916–Spring 1917,* 237.

8. Director's memos, 1918–1919, School of Music Records, RG #A1600, Louisiana State University Archives, LSU Libraries, Baton Rouge, LA.

9. *Reveille,* November 5, 1921.

10. Although the *Reveille* carried stories about the forthcoming events planned for the opening of the new stadium in 1924, neither the *Reveille* nor the Baton Rouge newspapers published any descriptions of the activities after they took place.

2. THE GOVERNOR AND HIS BAND, 1930–1940

1. *State Times,* October 21, 1931; *Advocate,* February 26, 1994.

2. *State Times,* November 4, 1932.

3. For other information about Carazo and Long, see Charlie Roberts, "The History of the Louisiana State University Band" (Ph.D. dissertation, Louisiana State University, 1966).

4. Marie Louise and Juliette Bonnette, "Dancing Darlings of LSU," *Register,* September 21, 1968. Marie Louise married J. R. Nelson of Baton Rouge and Juliette married Wade O. Martin, Jr., who would become the Louisiana secretary of state.

5. *Advocate,* February 26, 1994; "Lew Williams Holds Fond Memories of the Kingfish," *Sunday Advertiser,* August 29, 1993.

6. Continé conversation with Frank Wickes, and Frank B. Wickes Oral History Interviews, 2013.

7. Director's memo, February 13, 1941, School of Music Records, LSU Archives.

8. President Hodges to Comptroller, copies to Director of the School of Music Barrett Stout, Band Director James S. Fisher, and Dean of the University Fred C. Frey, October 15, 1943, Office of the Chancellor Records, RG #A0001, Louisiana State University Archives, LSU Libraries, Baton Rouge, LA.

3. THE WAR YEARS, 1941–1945

1. Memos, September 11, 1940, February 13, 1941, School of Music Records, LSU Archives.

2. *Advocate,* December 6, 1940.

3. Memo, February 13, 1941, School of Music Records, LSU Archives; *Reveille,* November 5, 1941.

4. *Reveille,* March 28, 1942.

5. *State Times,* November 25, 1942.

6. *Advocate,* January 16, 1942; *LSU Alumni News,* March 1942.

7. Memo, February 13, 1941, School of Music Records, LSU Archives; *Reveille,* December 15, 1942.

8. *Advocate,* October 7, 1990; *Sunday Advocate,* November 21, 1993; Stout to Hodges, February 24, 1944, and Director of Band William E. Koogler to Stout and Hodges, March 9, 1944, Office of the Chancellor Records, LSU Archives.

9. "Alumni Reunion," *Morning Advocate,* September 19, 1986.

10. Ibid.; *Advocate,* August 4, 1942.

11. *Reveille,* May 9, 1945.

4. A TALE OF TWO DIRECTORS, 1946–1964

1. *Sunday Advocate,* October 7, 1990; *LSU Alumni News,* December 1949.

2. Col. Perry C. Cole to President Hatcher, October 21, 1946, Office of the Chancellor Records, LSU Archives; "Tiger Band," mimeographed booklet, 1949, Band Department, School of Music Records, LSU Archives.

3. Continé conversations with Tom Tyra, 1960.

4. "Ballerinas to Make Debut on the Football Field," *Sunday Advocate,* August 30, 1959; "Tiger Band's Ballet Corps," *Morning Advocate,* September 3, 1959; "Golden Girls," *Advocate,* October 7, 1990; "Football and Ballet," *State Times,* October 8, 1990.

5. "Golden Girls' 50th Anniversary," *Morning Advocate,* October 25, 2009.

6. Continé conversations with Tyra, 1960; "Remember When," *Advocate,* December 21, 1977; "Fox Sports on Hand for Completion of Documentary," *Advocate,* September 6, 2006.

7. "Tiger Band's New Home," *Reveille,* September 24, 1959; "New Band Wing at LSU," *Advocate,* September 16, 1959.

8. "Hey Fightin' Tigers," composer, Cy Coleman; original lyrics, Carolyn Leigh; LSU lyrics, Gene Quaw; arranged for band, Tom Tyra.

9. *Reveille,* September 24, 1959; "Tiger Band Directed by Young Chicagoan," *Advocate,* September 16, 1959.

5. THE ALL AMERICAN COLLEGE TV BAND, 1964–1977

1. *Advocate,* August 3, 2004; *New Orleans Times-Picayune,* August 5, 2004; http://alt.obit uaries.narkive.com/o0pV2Hbq/william-f-swor-led-lsu-s-golden-band-from-tigerland.

2. Travel itineraries and band handbooks, Frank B. Wickes Papers.

3. Swor's speech to Alumni Band, Kappa Kappa Psi, Beta Gamma chapter records, 1967–1968; Band performances at football games files, 1949, 1964–1977; "Continuity Script," LSU vs. Rice, September 23, 1967, all in Band Department, School of Music Records, LSU Archives.

4. Travel itineraries and band handbooks, Wickes Papers; *Advocate,* December 9, 1975.

5. "Forty Years of Flags," *Advocate,* September 25, 2011.

6. *Daily Reveille,* December 15, 1970; *State Times,* December 30, 1970; *LSU Alumni News,* February 1971; LSU Board of Supervisors to Swor, March 31, 1971, Band Department, School of Music Records, LSU Archives; *State Times,* August 19, 1971.

7. *Bonham (TX) Daily Favorite,* September 18, 1966; *Houston Post,* September 27, 1966; *Atlanta News Report,* December 31, 1968.

8. *State Times,* August 19, 1971; John A. Hunter to Chancellor Taylor, September 15, 1971; Swor to Taylor, May 26, 1972; Swor to Everett Timm and Timm to Taylor, July 7, 1972; Taylor to Timm and Swor, July 11, 1972; Carl Maddox to Swor, March 14, 1973; Taylor to Maddox, April 20, 1973; Maddox to Taylor, April 27, 1973; Taylor to Swor, Timm, and Maddox, May 15, 1973; and Swor to Maddox, September 12, 1973, all in Band Department, School of Music Records, LSU Archives.

9. Taylor to Swor, Timm, and Maddox, May 15, 1973, Band Department, School of Music Records, LSU Archives.

10. Continé correspondence and conversation with John S. Butler, 2014.

6. THE BAND IN TRANSITION, 1978–1980

1. *Daily Reveille,* February 21, 1968; *Advocate,* December 14, 2011.

2. Rouse to Murrill, January 15, 1976; Rouse to Vice Chancellor for Administration Pesson, May 22, 1976; Rouse to Pesson, December 9, 1976, all in Office of the Chancellor Records, LSU Archives.

3. "Acting Band Director for the Past Year Named the University Director of Bands," *Advocate,* July 29, 1977.

4. "Continuity Script," LSU vs. Rice, September 23, 1967, Band Department, School of Music Records, LSU Archives.

5. Rouse to Murrill, April 12, 1977, and Murrill to Rouse, October 19, 1976, Office of the Chancellor Records, LSU Archives. Title VI, 42 U.S.C. § 2000d et seq., was enacted as part of the Civil Rights Act of 1964. It prohibits discrimination on the basis of race, color, and national origin in programs and activities receiving federal financial assistance.

6. Timm to Murrill, June 11, 1979, March 7, 18, 1980; Rouse to Murrill, April 12, 1977; Victor Klimash reports to Murrill, August 28, 1979, all in Office of the Chancellor Records, LSU Archives.

7. *Advocate,* August 22, 1986, August 15, 1988, December 26, 1993.

7. THE WICKES YEARS, 1980–2010

1. All information in this chapter attributed to Frank Wickes comes from the Frank B. Wickes Oral History Interviews, September 30, October 15, 22, 30, 2013, in T. Harry Williams Center for Oral History, LSU Libraries, Baton Rouge, LA.

2. Black Greeks representative Andrea Stump and Student Government Association Black Affairs chairman Cedric Floyd to Murrill, March 7, 1980; Randy Lopez, Director, LSU Equal Opportunity Programs, to Robert F. Shambaugh, Acting Dean, School of Music, March 12, 1980; J. J. McKernan, LSU Board of Supervisors, to Murrill, March 18, 1980; Lopez to Murrill, March 25, 1980, all in Office of the Chancellor Records, LSU Archives.

3. *Morning Advocate,* April 3, 1989.

4. Ibid.

5. Ibid., October 5, 1985.

6. *Daily Reveille,* March 6, 1986.

7. "Alumni Reunion," *Morning Advocate,* September 19, 1986; "Band Reunion," *LSU Magazine,* LSU Alumni Association, Baton Rouge, LA, November 1986.

8. *Advocate,* November 30, 1987.

9. *Advocate Sunday Magazine,* March 10, 1991.

10. "Performing in Nation's Capital," *Advocate Sunday Magazine,* January 30, 1994; *Kennedy Center Stagebill,* February 1994; *Advocate,* Washington Bureau, February 10, 1994.

11. *Morning Advocate,* April 3, 1989.

12. *Jennings (LA) Daily News,* September 26, 1999.

13. John Philip Sousa Foundation, Sudler Trophy, www.sousafoundation.net.

14. Louisiana Music Hall of Fame http://louisianamusichalloffame.org.

15. *Advocate,* October 7, 1990, October 19, 2009.

8. THE TRADITION CONTINUES

1. *Advocate Sunday Magazine,* December 23, 2007; *Advocate,* January 23, 2009.

2. Continé interview with Stephen Koivisto, fall 2014.

3. Continé interview with Mary Bahlinger, fall 2014.

4. *Advocate,* February 12, 2011.

5. Continé conversations with Roy King, 2014; *Advocate,* March 17, 2014; Chelsea Brasted, "Tiger Band to March in 2014 St. Patrick's Day Parade in Dublin, Ireland," *Times-Picayune,* www.nola.com; www.stpatricsfestival.le.

NOTE ON SOURCES

PRIMARY SOURCES

Historical research sources on administration, organization, development, students, facilities, policies, and photographs relating to the LSU Band from 1893 through 2014 were found in a number of record groups within the Louisiana State University Archives, LSU Libraries. Particularly important are:

Department of Military Sciences Records, RG #A0302
LSU Photograph Collection, RG #A5000
    Band Department Football Performance Photographs, RG #A5000.1601
    Jack Fiser Photographs, RG #A5000.0020.1
Office of the Chancellor Records, RG #A0001
Office of Public Relations Records, RG #A0020
School of Music Records, RG #A1600

Also valuable are the LSU Band Department Files, held in the department offices on campus.

The Frank B. Wickes Papers, an extensive resource, are still held by Mr. Wickes. All information attributed to Frank B. Wickes in chapter 7 comes from the Frank B. Wickes Oral History Interviews, September 30, October 15, 22, and 30, 2013, T. Harry Williams Center for Oral History, LSU Libraries. The Russell B. Long Collection, Mss. 3700, Louisiana and Lower Mississippi Valley Collections, LSU Libraries, contains numerous band photographs.

SECONDARY SOURCES

LOUISIANA STATE UNIVERSITY PUBLICATIONS
Gumbo
LSU Alumni News
LSU Catalog
LSU Magazine
Reveille

NEWSPAPERS
Louisiana
    Baton Rouge Advocate
    Baton Rouge State Times
    Jennings Daily News
    New Orleans Times-Picayune
    Sunday Advertiser (Baton Rouge)
Tennessee
    Memphis Commercial Appeal
Texas
    Bonham Daily Favorite
    Houston Post

WEBSITES (LAST ACCESSED JULY 27, 2015):
John Philip Sousa Foundation. "The Sudler Trophy." www.sousafoundation.net.
Louisiana Music Hall of Fame. http://louisianamusichalloffame.org.
St. Patrick's Day Parade in Dublin, Ireland. www.stpatricsfestival.le.

A NOTE ON THE PHOTOGRAPHS

Many of the photographs appearing in this book have long credit lines. In an effort to improve readability, we devised a shorthand reference system. A key to their sources is listed below:

BDFP   Office of Public Relations Records, Band Department Football Perform-ance Photographs, RG #A5000.1601, Louisiana State University Archives, LSU Libraries, Baton Rouge, Louisiana.

DMS   Department of Military Science Records, RG #A0302, Louisiana State University Archives, LSU Libraries, Baton Rouge, Louisiana.

JFP   Office of Public Relations Records, Jack Fiser Photographs, RG #A5000.0020.1, Louisiana State University Archives, LSU Libraries, Baton Rouge, Louisiana.

LLMVC   Louisiana and Lower Mississippi Valley Collections, LSU Libraries.

LSU Band   LSU Band Department Files.

LSUPC   LSU Photograph Collection, RG #A5000, Louisiana State University Archives, LSU Libraries, Baton Rouge, Louisiana.

OPRR   Office of Public Relations Records, RG #A0020, Louisiana State University Archives, LSU Libraries, Baton Rouge, Louisiana.

RBL   Russell B. Long Papers, Mss. 3700, Louisiana and Lower Mississippi Valley Collections, LSU Libraries, Baton Rouge, Louisiana.

A NOTE
ON *THE GOLDEN BAND FROM TIGERLAND*

Large universities with strong athletic programs, especially in the Deep South, attract a following that goes beyond alumni and current students, and reaches into the realm of "fandom." Louisiana State University is certainly part of that group of schools. Football, tailgating, and the traditions that surround those activities are legendary as well as essential elements of the LSU experience, whether you are a student, an alum, or someone that just happens to love the LSU Tigers.

We cannot think about the vibrant traditions surrounding LSU football without calling to mind the band. LSU's Golden Band from Tigerland is the heartbeat of Game Day, and its songs and cheers are the battle cries of that legion of fans. Its story is a fascinating one, ably told here by Tom Continé and Faye Phillips. Beginning as a small but dedicated group of cadets in the 1890s, the LSU Band has evolved into the spectacular 325-member organization we see and hear today.

As an archivist, I have a special appreciation for the history of the university that touches on all of these things, and much more. LSU Libraries' Special Collections is responsible for documenting, preserving, and making accessible all sorts of material that records the history and culture of Louisiana State University, from its founding through today. We take this responsibility seriously and invite visitors to use materials, participate in events, view exhibits, and peruse our online holdings.

This book is just one brilliant example of what can result when that invitation is accepted. We provide the raw material that facilitates telling a story. In the case of this book, the authors used a broad array of resources from Special Collections at Hill Memorial Library. The LSU student newspaper, the *Reveille,* was also a part of the research, as was the LSU yearbook, the *Gumbo.* Other resources include photographs, oral histories from the T. Harry Williams Center for Oral History (whose collections are housed at Hill), and a myriad of LSU's archival records, including extensive use of materials from the LSU School of Music and the Office of the Chancellor.

Archives represent, reflect, and provide documentary evidence about the lives and the work of our fellow human beings, from senators to farmers, from famous authors to housewives, from civic leaders to ordinary citizens. As with the Golden Band from Tigerland, a group of individuals working together can create something greater than the sum of the parts. Countless stories like that of the LSU Band are in the Archives, waiting to be discovered, interpreted, and told.

—Jessica Lacher-Feldman
Head, Special Collections
LSU Libraries

INDEX